2015

中国旅行社行业发展研究报告

RESEARCH REPORT ON THE DEVELOPMENT OF TRAVEL AGENCY IN CHINA (2015)

中华人民共和国国家旅游局 编

中国旅游出版社

2015中国旅行社行业发展研究报告

编委员会名单

前　言

旅行社是旅游业的龙头，是促进旅游产业发展的重要生产力，也是连接旅游生产服务各个环节的纽带和沟通旅游生产、消费的桥梁，在推动旅游消费、增加社会就业、促进人民交流等方面发挥着积极作用。

随着大众旅游的不断深入，旅行社产业的规模和产出在不断扩大。截至 2014 年年底，全国旅行社统计调查系统共有 26650 家完成了 2014 年经营数据的填报，共拥有资产 1292.97 亿元，创造营业收入 4029.59 亿元，上缴营业税金及附加 16.60 亿元，所得税 7.56 亿元，提供了 34.13 万个就业岗位。

为更好地让全社会了解旅行社产业发展的现状，分析产业面临的问题，研究产业发展的趋势，国家旅游局从 2015 年开始在旅行社统计基础上编制《中国旅行社行业发展研究报告》，分四章对我国旅行社行业的发展现状、发展特点、发展趋势进行了阐述和分析。本书可供行业管理者、从业人员和相关研究人员学习参考。在此，要感谢所有提供相关数据的旅行社，感谢各级旅游行政管理部门的汇总和审核。

不足之处，欢迎批评指正。

编者

二〇一五年十二月一日

目 录

Part I 2015 中国旅行社行业发展研究报告

Part Ⅱ　Research Report on the Development of Travel Agency in China（2015）

Part Ⅲ 附 录

Part I

2015 中国旅行社行业发展研究报告

第一章

我国旅行社行业发展现状

一、2014 年旅行社行业发展回顾

1. 旅行社总量增长，增速逐年下降

截至 2014 年年底，全国旅行社总数为 26650 家，同比增长 2.29%。2002 年以来，全国旅行社总量增长率呈现出波动下行的态势，2010 年以后各年的增长率均在 5% 左右徘徊，2014 年更是达到历史新低。但从地区上看，东部经济发达、创新活跃的省份，以及中西部特别重视发展旅游业的省份的旅行社数量还是有较大幅度增长，2014 年增长最多的省份增幅达 20%。

2. 旅行社资产规模增长，增速持续走高

2014 年度，全国旅行社资产合计为 1292.97 亿元，同比增长 24.35%，其中，负债 848.12 亿元，同比增长 21.65%；所有者权益 444.85 亿元，同比增长 29.84%。自 2011 年以来，全国旅行社资产总额增长快速，增长率持续走高，越来越多的传统旅行社开始主动寻求与资本市场融合发展，同时资本市场对行业也投入了更多的热情。

3. 旅游业务营业收入增长，增速略有回升

2014 年度全国旅行社旅游业务营业收入 3398.05 亿元，同比增长 6.54%，占营业收入的 84.33%。2014 年是《旅游法》实施的第二年，传统旅行社业在运作理念、组织模式上也在不断尝试创新，以适应消费市场变化和法制时代的到来，团队游客对旅行社提供的旅游服务满意度有所提升。全年旅游业务营业收入与 2013 年相比有较快增长。

4. 旅游业务利润增长，增速连续下降

2014 年度，全国旅行社旅游业务利润 170.32 亿元，同比增长 4.96%。由于成本上升和市场竞争加剧等因素影响，全国旅行社旅游业务利润总额尽管在数量上一直处于上涨态势，但其增速连续两年下降，2014 年相较 2012 年的 11.82% 下降了 6.86 个百分点。

5. 旅行社利税增长，增速稳中有升

2014 年度全国旅行社实缴税金 24.16 亿元，同比增长 8.00%。从历史数据看，2004 ~ 2010 年，全国旅行社实缴税金呈现高速增长的态势，2010 年达到历史最高的 55.29%，2011 年后各年趋缓。值得关注的是，2014 年全国旅行社实缴税金的增长率较 2013 年的 2.29% 上升了 5.71 个百分点。

6. 旅行社就业稳定，高学历人员比重不断攀升

2014 年度，全国旅行社直接从业人员 341312 人，同比增长 0.39%，其中大专以上学历 243393 人，同比增长 2.13%。自 2002 年开始，全国旅行社从业人员数量始终处于增长状态。自 2010 年以来，拥有大专以上学历的旅游从业人员数量占从业人员总数的比重不断攀升，从 2010 年的 61.63% 到 2014 年的 71.31%，增幅近 10%。

二、2014 年旅行社市场特点分析

1. 旅行社的外延正在经历被动扩充的历史阶段

随着互联网的迅猛发展，在线旅游业务快速渗透。酒店和机票是最先被在线化的旅游产品品类，此外，旅游度假产品、租车、景区门票、签证等产品进入了快速在线化的进程。这些业务的经营主体，使得过去未纳入旅行社类别的多种旅游服务机构开始进入旅游服务业的范畴，传统旅行社的业务不断被新兴产业主体侵蚀，旅行社的外延正在经历被动扩充的历史阶段。

2. 旅行社三大市场呈现“两升一降”的阶段特点

2014 年，在全球经济缓慢复苏和国内宏观经济企稳的背景下，我国旅游经济顶住下行压力，旅游市场“两升一降”。在宏观经济企稳和旅游日益成为老百姓常态化生活方式的背景下，国内旅游消费需求保持平稳增长态势；由于全球经济尚未完全从金融危机中复苏，我国旅游价格竞争力减弱，各国和地区加大对旅游客源的争夺力度，加上我国入境旅游市场进入成熟阶段，以及大范围雾霾天气、环境污染等多重因素的影响，我国入境旅游复苏乏力；在国内经济社会发展良好基本面的支撑下，加上人民币升值、各国和各地区纷纷推出便利化政策等因素的影响，我国出境旅游继续快速增长，但增长率呈回落态势。

2014 年度全国旅行社国内旅游营业收入 1783.68 亿元，同比增长 1.22%，占全国旅行社旅游业务营业收入总量的 52.49%；2014 年度全国旅行社出境旅游营业收入 1331.33 亿元，同比增长 15.05%，占全国旅行社旅游业务营业收入总量的 39.18%；2014 年度全国旅行社入境旅游营业收入 283.04 亿元，同比增长 4.77%，占全国旅行社旅游业务营业收入总量的 8.11%。

3. 资本市场成为传统旅行社产业转型升级的助推力量

在当前旅游行业激烈竞争的历史阶段，资本已经成为重要的竞争性要素，逐步成为商业模式创新及建构的重要推手，为传统产业升级提供了助推力量。2014 年，众信收购竹园国旅；携程与中信联合控股华远旅游；途牛收购经典假期和中山国旅；

万达旅业也加紧收购步伐，仅2014年一年就收购了12家线下传统旅行社。资本市场的持续关注和热捧，加快了传统旅行社行业转方式、调结构的步伐，更好地适应市场变化，真正着眼于满足游客在旅行过程中的核心诉求。

4. 旅行社国内旅游市场稳步增长，比重下降

随着旅游消费者的日渐成熟、旅游消费习惯的变化以及私家车的增多和道路交通建设的快速进步，散客市场的迅猛增长，依靠旅行社的团队旅游市场在不断萎缩。全国来看，从2009～2013年，旅行社组织的国内旅游人次在国内旅游总人次中比重下降明显，5年的百分比分别仅为5.31%、5.71%、5.19%、4.87%和3.95%。2014年上半年，全国旅行社国内旅游组织1873.91万人次，占比仅为2.8%，旅行社组织的团队旅游市场在国内旅游市场中的地位仍在持续下降。

5. 旅行社行业存在较大的区域不平衡性

无论是从旅行社数量，还是从旅行社经营的各项指标来看，全国旅行社行业发展都存在着较大的区域不平衡性，其中华东地区表现最为抢眼，其次为华北和华南地区，西北、西南、东北地区发展相对滞后。从旅行社数量上看，2014年华东地区的旅行社数量占全国总量的37.43%，华北地区占比为17.56%；而西北地区和西南地区的旅行社数量仅占全国总量的7.75%和7.10%。从旅行社旅游业务经营收入这项指标来看，2014年度华东地区旅行社旅游业务营业收入占全国总数的39.84%，华北地区占比18.06%；而西北地区、东北地区占比仅为3.14%和4.78%，合计占比不足10%。

第二章

我国旅行社行业规模及经营情况

一、旅行社数量及规模

1. 全国旅行社数量

截至 2014 年年底，全国旅行社总数为 26650 家，同比增长 2.29%。从各省（直辖市、自治区）的增长情况看，四川、河南、湖南等 10 个省份旅行社数量减少，减幅最大的四川为 22.01%；重庆、海南、西藏、新疆生产建设兵团等 4 个省份旅行社数量持平；其余 18 个省份旅行社数量都有不同程度的增长，增幅最大的宁夏为 20%，另有北京和云南 2 个省份增长超过 10%。

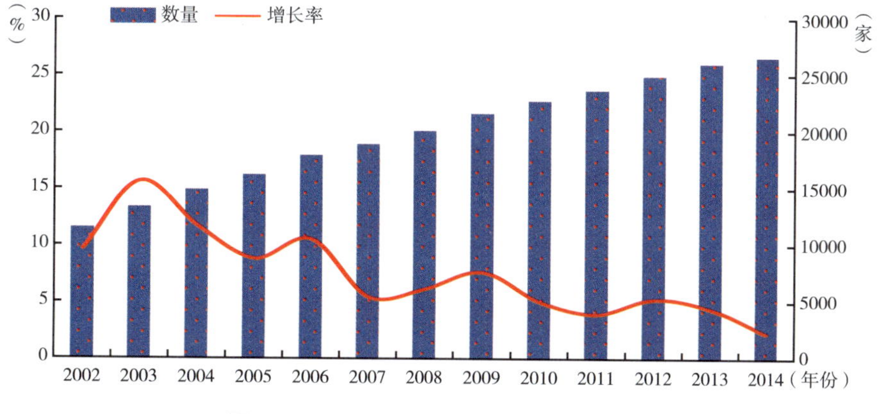

图 2-1　2002 ~ 2014 年全国旅行社数量

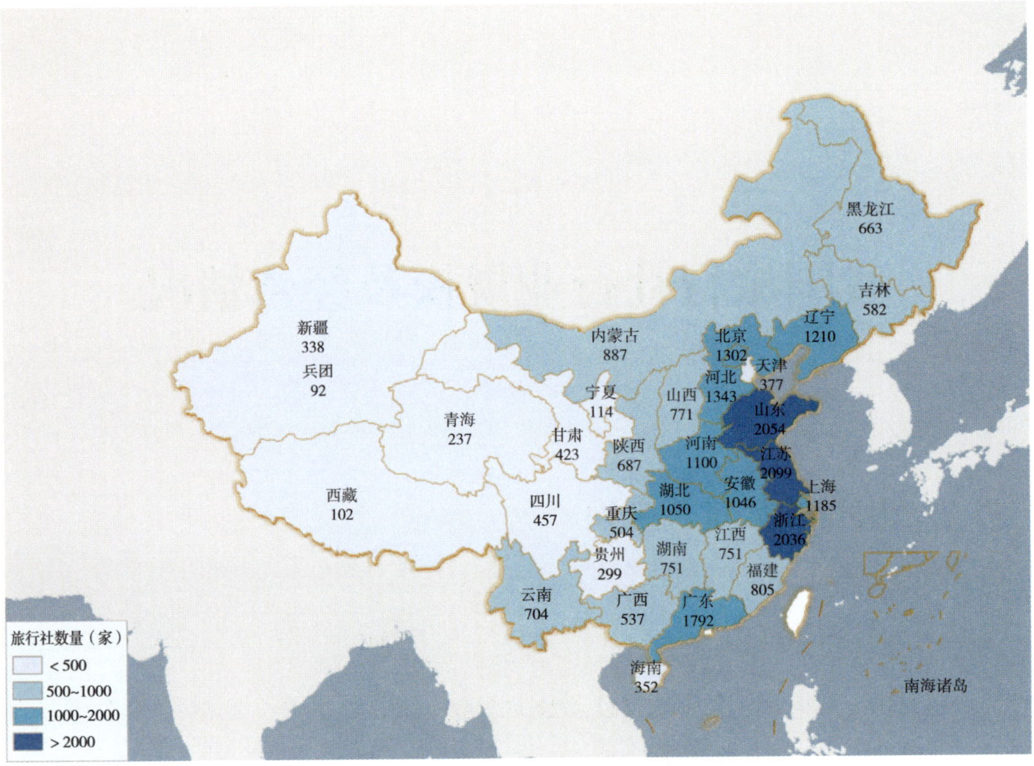

图 2–2　2014 年全国各地旅行社数量分布

地图来源：国家测绘局网站，审图号：GS（2014）6070 号

随着大众旅游的兴起，休假制度的不断改革，国人对旅游服务的需求不断增长，自 2002 年以来，全国旅行社总量一直处于增长状态。但由于技术的进步和大众消费模式的变迁等因素的影响，传统旅行社业的发展空间被不断地挤压，其增长率近年来呈现出波动下行的态势，2010 年以后各年的增长率均在 5% 左右徘徊，2014 年更是达到历史新低。

2. 全国旅行社资产规模

全国旅行社资产合计为 1292.97 亿元，同比增长 24.35%，其中，负债 848.12 亿元，同比增长 21.65%；所有者权益 444.85 亿元，同比增长 29.84%。自 2002 年以来，全国旅行社资产总额总体呈波动增长趋势，几个下降的节点均为受到不可抗力的影响，如 2003 年上半年“非典”疫情，2005 年禽流感肆虐，2008 年席卷全球的金融危机等，除此之外，其余年份全国旅行社资产总额均有所上升。在经历了2009年和2010年两年两位数高速增长后，2011年稍有回落。2011年之后，全国旅行社资产总额增长快速，增长率持续走高。2014年，“民营旅行社第一股”众信旅游IPO后连续多次涨停，中青旅、中国国旅等也受到资本市场的热捧，越来越多的传统旅行社开始主动寻求与资本市场融合发展，积极应对挑战。

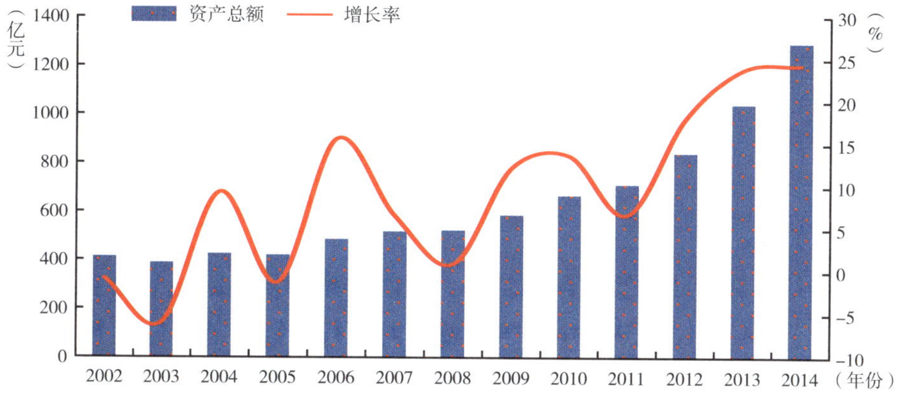

图2-3　2002～2014年全国旅行社资产总额

3. 全国七大分区数量分布

2014年，华北地区共有旅行社4680家，占全国旅行社总数的17.56%；东北地区共有旅行社2455家，占全国旅行社总数的9.21%；华东地区共有旅行社9976家，占全国旅行社总数的37.43%；华南地区共有旅行社2681家，占全国旅行社总数的10.06%；华中地区共有旅行社2901家，占全国旅行社总数的10.89%；西北地区（包括兵团）共有旅行社1891家，占全国旅行社总数的7.10%。

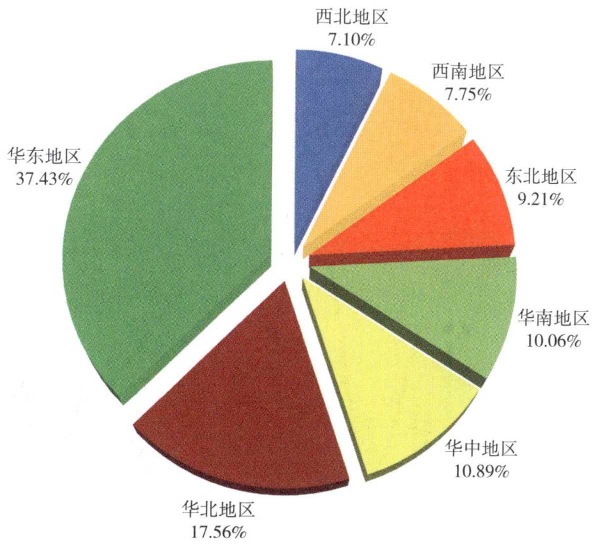

图2-4　2014年度全国七大分区旅行社数量分布

二、旅游业务营业收入

1. 全国旅行社旅游业务营业收入

2014 年度全国旅行社旅游业务营业收入 3398.05 亿元，同比增长 6.54%，占营业收入的 84.33%。2002 ~ 2010 年，除 2003 年、2005 年、2008 年等特殊年份，全国旅行社旅游业务营业收入一直处于增长状态。因为这些特殊年份的存在，全国旅行社旅游业务营业收入的增长率呈现出剧烈波动状态。2010 年以来，受经济大环境不景气、众多行业广受牵连的影响，全国旅行社旅游业务营业收入增速呈波动下行态势。

2014 年是《旅游法》实施的第二年，依法兴旅和依法治旅取得重要进展，经过完善旅游监管和治理市场秩序，团队游客对旅行社提供的旅游服务满意度大大提升，创历史新高。传统旅行社业在运作理念、组织模式上也在不断尝试创新，以适应消费市场变化和法制时代的到来，2014 年旅游业务营业收入与 2013 年相比有较快增长。

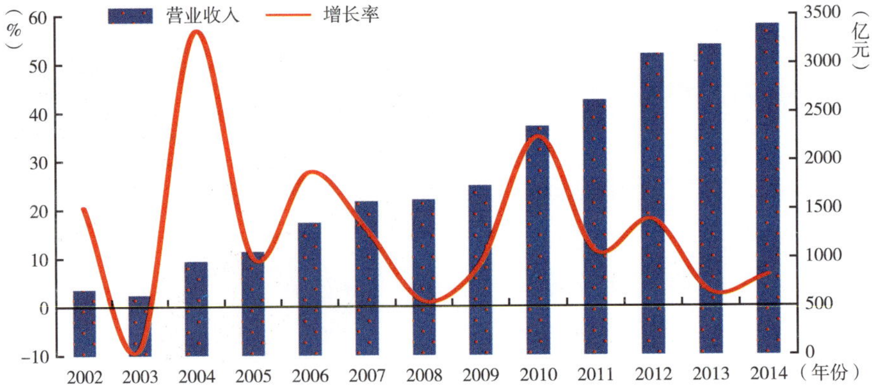

图 2-5　2002 ~ 2014 年全国旅行社旅游业务营业收入总额

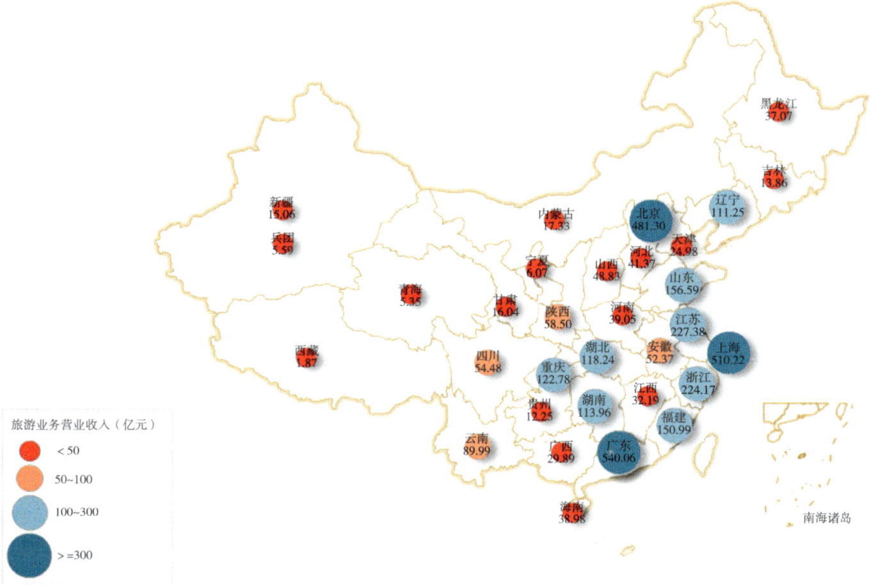

图 2–6　2014 年度全国各地旅行社旅游业务营业收入分布

地图来源：国家测绘局网站，审图号：GS（2014）6070 号

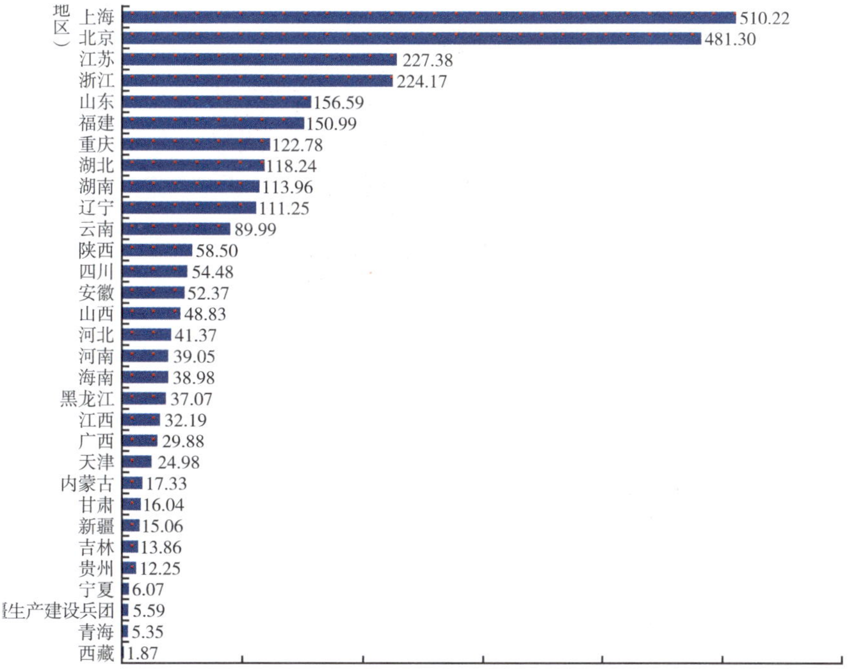

图 2–7　2014 年度全国各地旅行社旅游业务营业收入

2. 全国七大分区旅游业务营业收入分布

2014 年度华北地区旅行社旅游业务营业收入 613.81 亿元，占全国旅行社旅游业务营业收入总数的 18.06%；东北地区旅行社旅游业务营业收入 162.18 亿元，占全国旅行社旅游业务营业收入总数的 4.77%；华东地区旅行社旅游业务营业收入 1353.90 亿元，占全国旅行社旅游业务营业收入总数的 39.84%；华南地区旅行社旅游业务营业收入 608.91 亿元，占全国旅行社旅游业务营业收入总数的 17.92%；华中地区旅行社旅游业务营业收入 271.25 亿元，占全国旅行社旅游业务营业收入总数的 7.98%；西南地区旅行社旅游业务营业收入 281.38 亿元，占全国旅行社旅游业务营业收入总数的 8.28%；西北地区（包括新疆生产建设兵团）旅行社旅游业务营业收入 106.61 亿元，占全国旅行社旅游业务营业收入总数的 3.14%。

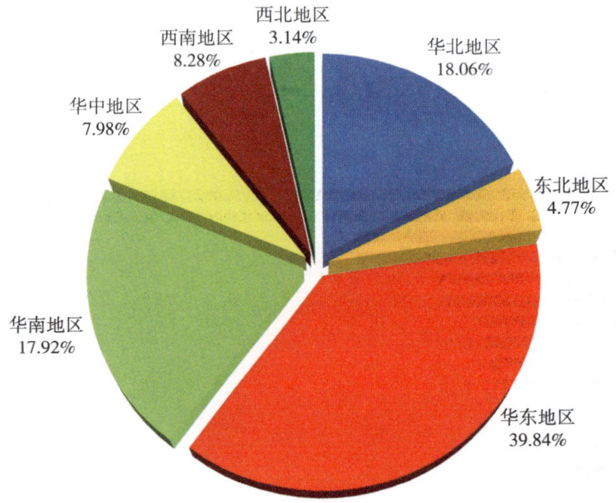

图 2-8　2014 年度全国七大分区旅行社旅游业务营业收入分布

三、旅游业务利润

1. 全国旅行社旅游业务利润

2014 年，全国旅行社旅游业务利润 170.32 亿元，同比增长 4.96%。自 2004 年起，旅行社旅游业务利润在数量上呈现持续上涨态势，但其增长率除在 2005 年、2008 年等特殊年份的次年出现增长外，一直处于下降的状态。2011 年较 2010 年略微上扬。自 2012 年以来，由于成本上升和市场竞争加剧等因素影响，全国旅行社旅游业务的利润呈现新一轮下降态势。2014 年全国旅行社旅游业务利润总额增长缓慢，增速为近三年来最低。

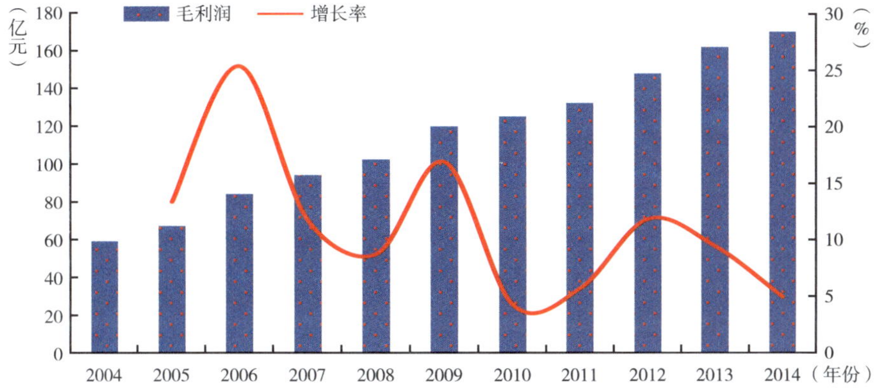

图 2-9　2004～2014 年全国旅行社旅游业务利润总额

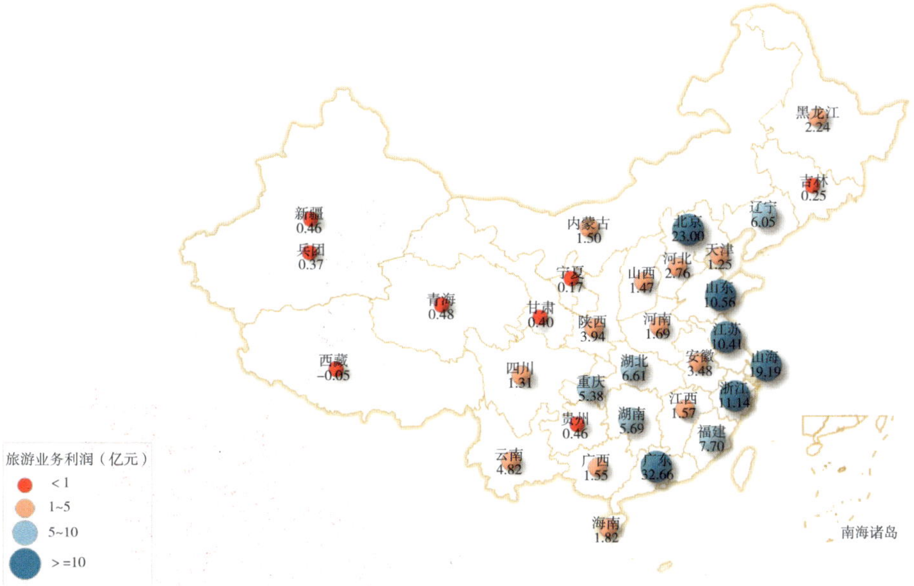

图 2-10　2014 年度全国各地旅行社旅游业务利润分布

地图来源：国家测绘局网站，审图号：GS（2014）6070 号

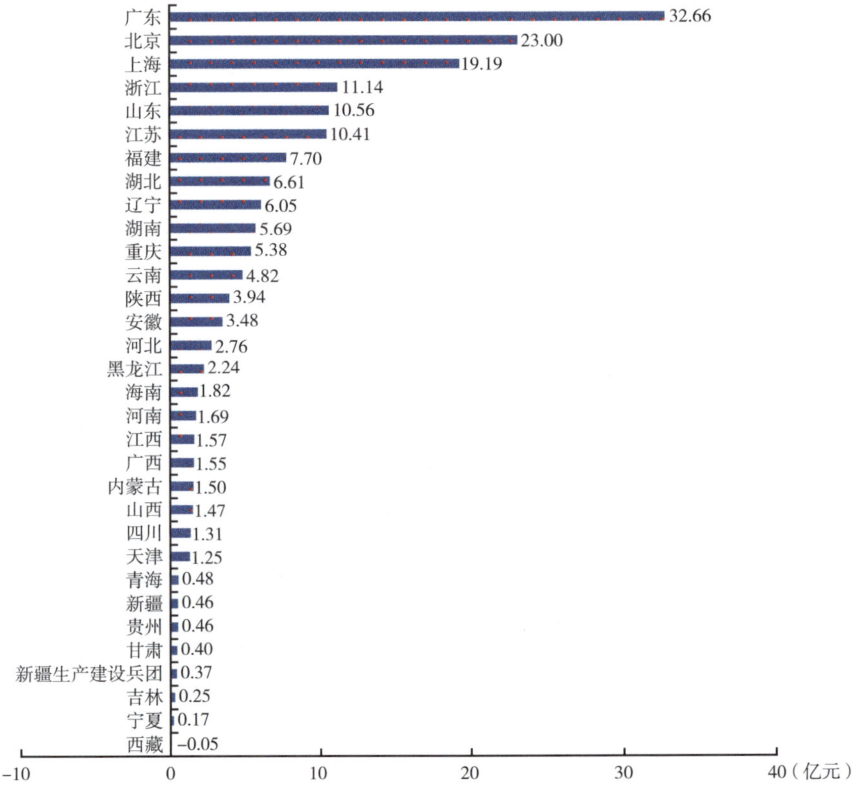

图 2-11　2014 年度全国各地旅行社旅游业务利润

2. 全国七大分区旅游业务利润分布

2014 年度华北地区旅行社旅游业务利润 29.98 亿元，占全国旅行社旅游业务利润总数的 17.60%；东北地区旅行社旅游业务利润 8.54 亿元，占全国旅行社旅游业务利润总数的 5.01%；华东地区旅行社旅游业务利润 64.05 亿元，占全国旅行社旅游业务利润总数

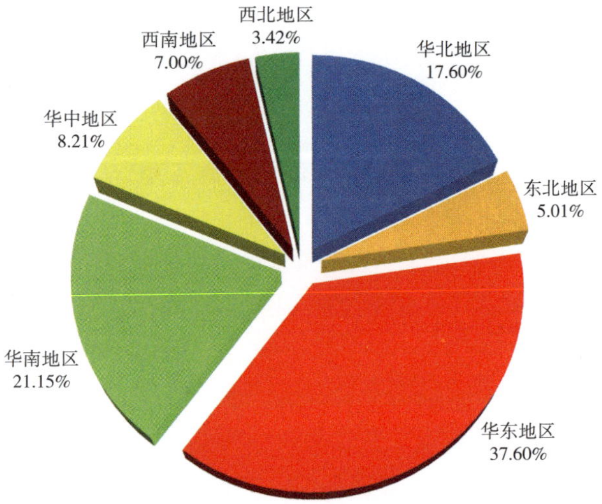

图 2-12　2014 年度全国七大分区旅行社旅游业务利润分布

的 37.60%；华南地区旅行社旅游业务利润 36.02 亿元，占全国旅行社旅游业务利润总数的 21.15%；华中地区旅行社旅游业务利润 13.99 亿元，占全国旅行社旅游业务利润总数的 8.21%；西南地区旅行社旅游业务利润 11.91 亿元，占全国旅行社旅游业务利润总数的 7.00%；西北地区（包括新疆生产建设兵团）旅行社旅游业务利润 5.82 亿元，占全国旅行社旅游业务利润总数的 3.42%。

四、实缴税金

1. 全国旅行社实缴税金

2014 年度全国旅行社实缴税金 24.16 亿元，同比增长 8.00%。旅行社实缴税金的数量和增长率波动情况，与旅行社营业收入和利润是息息相关的，其总体态势也与之颇为相似。从历年的情况看，2004 年以来，全国旅行社实缴税金一直呈现高速增长的态势，即使 2005 年这个特殊的年份，增长仍达到 16.82%，2008 年也有 2.89% 的增长。全国旅行社实缴税金的增长率在 2010 年达到历史最高后，于 2011 年大幅缩水，其后各年趋缓。

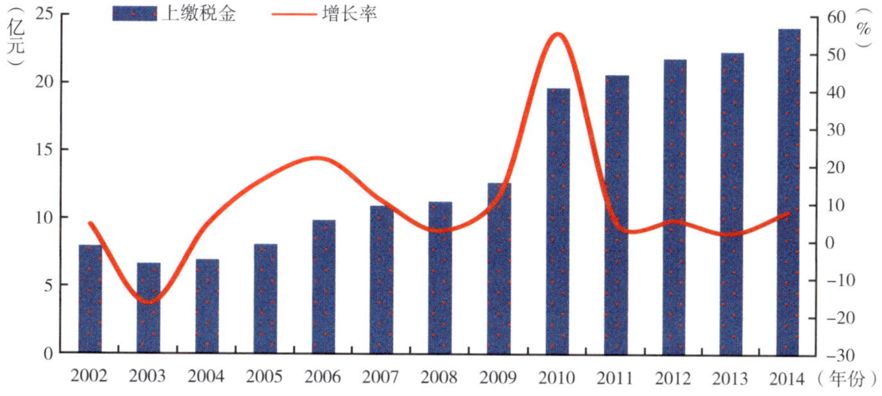

图 2-13　2002 ~ 2014 年全国旅行社实缴税金总额

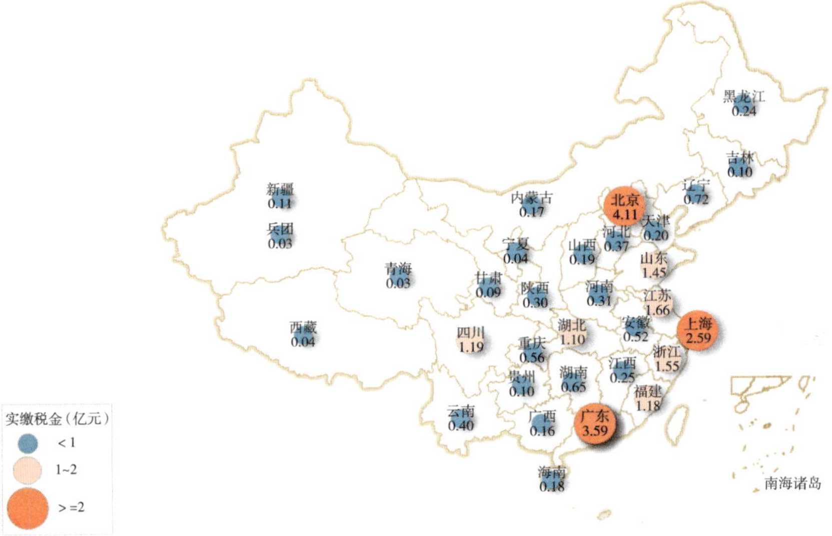

图 2-14　2014 年度全国各地旅行社实缴税金分布

地图来源：国家测绘局网站，审图号：GS（2014）6070 号

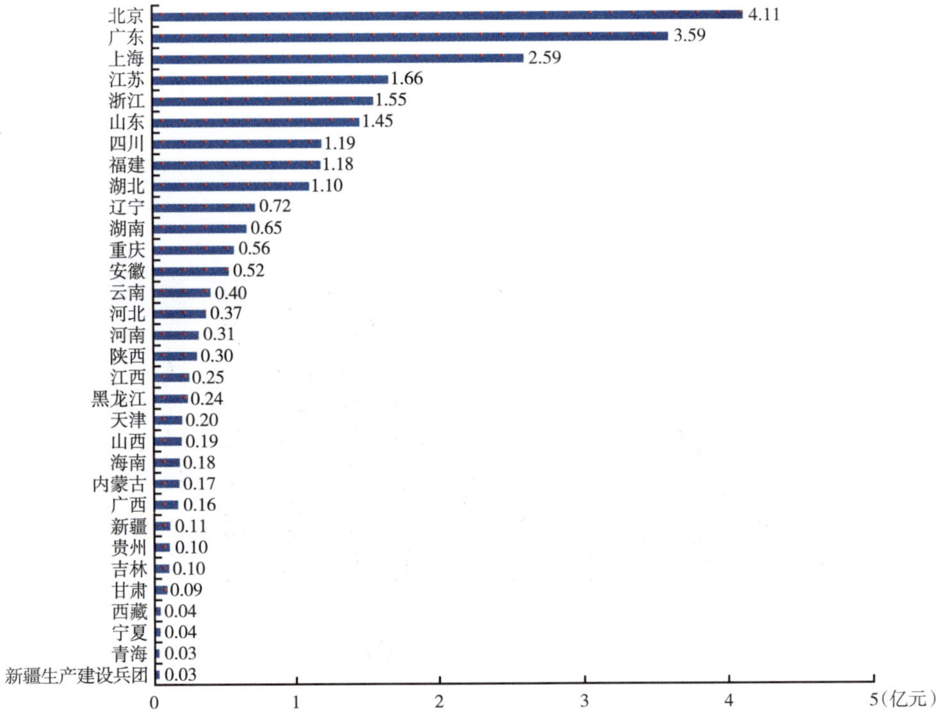

图 2-15　2014 年度全国各地旅行社实缴税金

2. 全国七大分区实缴税金分布

2014 年度华北地区旅行社实缴税金 5.04 亿元，占全国旅行社实缴税金总数的 20.84%；东北地区旅行社实缴税金 1.05 亿元，占全国旅行社实缴税金总数的 4.35%；华东地区旅行社实缴税金 9.21 亿元，占全国旅行社实缴税金总数的 38.12%；华南地区旅行社实缴税金 3.93 亿元，占全国旅行社实缴税金总数的 16.26%；华中地区旅行社实缴税金 2.07 亿元，占全国旅行社实缴税金总数的 8.55%；西南地区旅行社实缴税金 2.29 亿元，占全国旅行社实缴税金总数的 9.46%；西北地区旅行社实缴税金 0.59 亿元，占全国旅行社实缴税金总数的 2.42%。

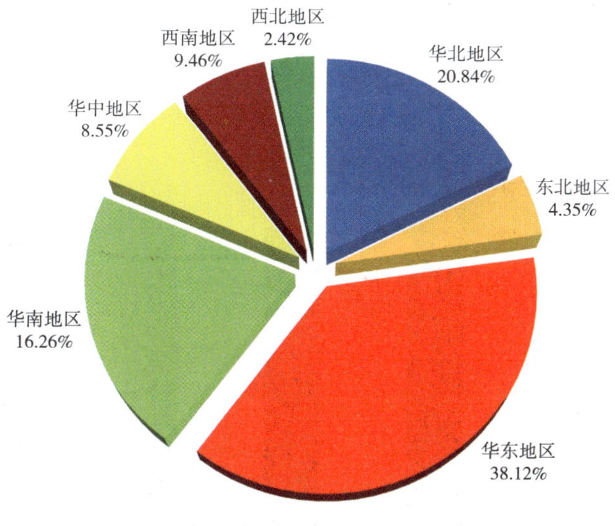

图 2-16 2014 年度全国七大分区旅行社实缴税金分布

五、人力资源情况

2014 年，全国旅行社直接从业人员 341312 人，同比增长 0.39%。其中大专以上学历 243393 人，同比增长 2.13%。值得关注的是，自 2010 年以来，拥有大专以上学历的旅游从业人员数量占从业人员总数的比重不断攀升，从 2010 年的 61.63%

到 2014 年的 71.31%，增幅近 10%，由此可见，越来越多接受过高等教育和专业培训的人才进入到旅行社行业中来，这是行业转型升级的需要，更是市场的需要。

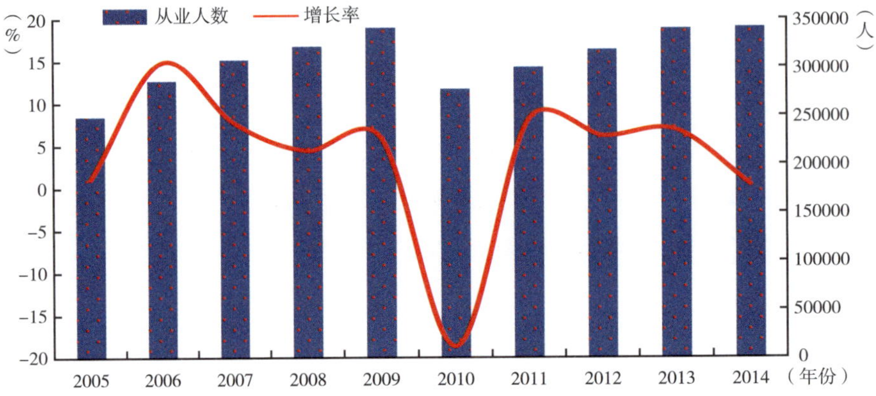

图 2-17　2005～2014 年全国旅行社直接从业人员总数

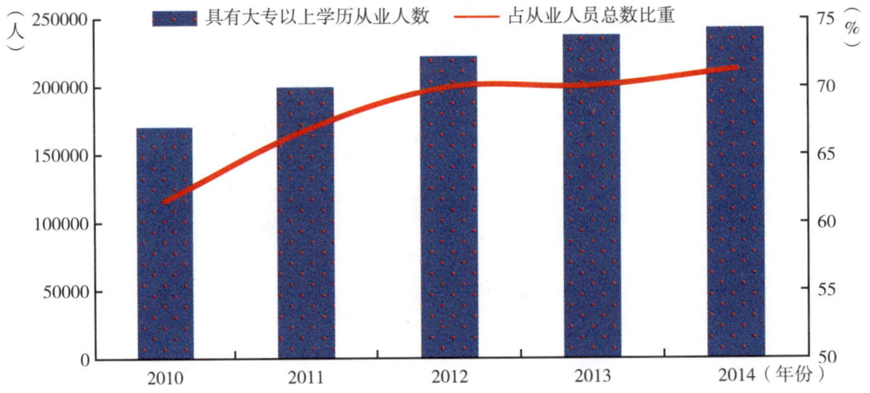

图 2-18　2010～2014 年全国旅行社具有大专以上学历从业人员总数

第三章

我国旅行社行业分项业务分析

一、国内旅游业务

2014 年度全国旅行社国内旅游组织 13116.66 万人次、41545.83 万人天，接待 14457.77 万人次、34978.44 万人天，分别同比增长 2.03%、1.72%，减少 0.43%、增长 3.40%。

2014 年，全国旅行社国内旅游的组织接待情况较 2013 年有所好转，但增长依然缓慢，其中接待人次指标更是持续减少。相较于国内旅游人次两位数的增长，以上数据说明越来越多的国内旅游者选择自由行而非跟随旅行社出行。

图 3–1　2002 ~ 2014 年全国旅行社组织国内旅游人次数及增长率

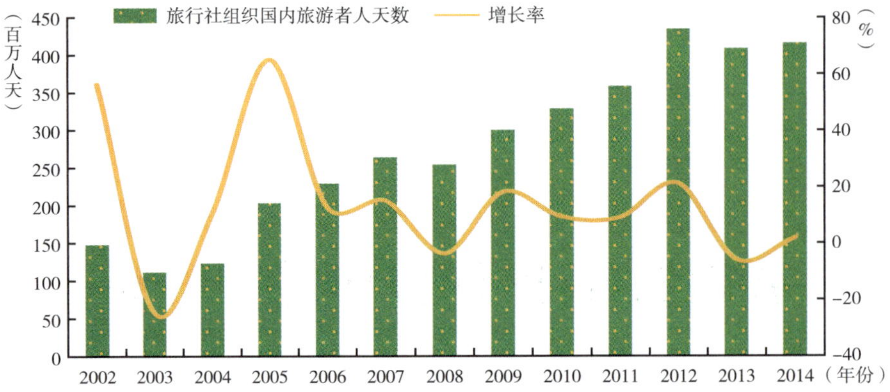

图 3-2　2002～2014 年全国旅行社组织国内旅游人天数及增长率

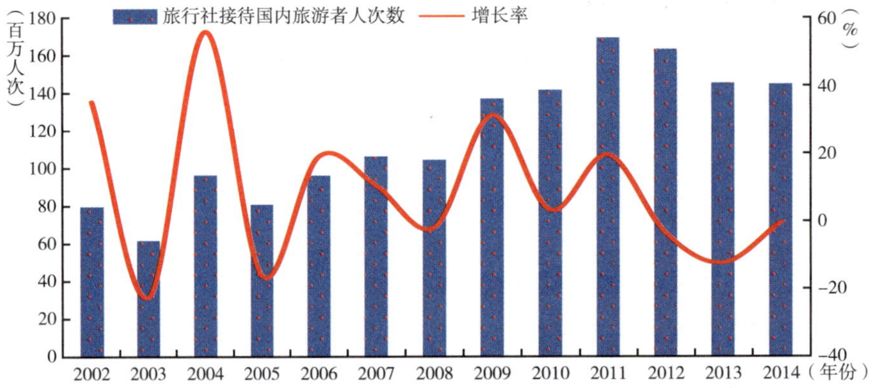

图 3-3　2002～2014 年全国旅行社接待国内旅游人次及增长率

图 3-4　2002～2014 年全国旅行社接待国内旅游人天数及增长率

2014年度旅行社国内旅游组织人次排名前十位的省（直辖市、自治区）依次为广东、江苏、浙江、山东、上海、湖北、重庆、福建、辽宁、湖南。

2014年，北京跌出国内旅游组织人次排名前十，代替它的是新晋上位的辽宁，广东虽份额稍降，但依然稳居首位，前三名的组成无变化。

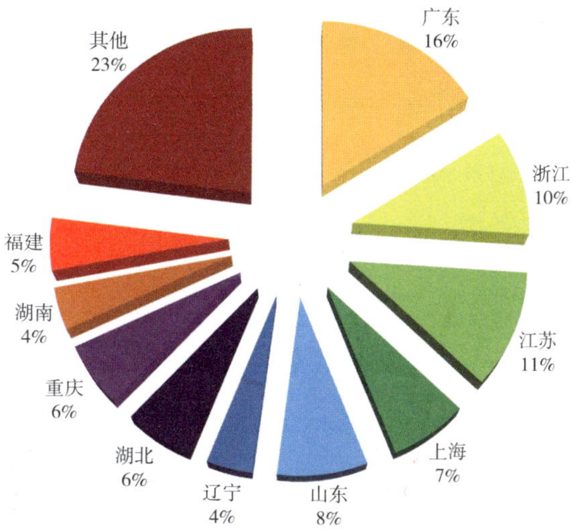

图3-5　2014年度国内旅游组织人次排名前十位的地区情况

2014年度旅行社国内旅游接待人次排名前十位的省（直辖市、自治区）依次为江苏、浙江、广东、福建、湖北、山东、云南、重庆、上海、四川。

2014年，四川取代湖南重回国内旅游接待人次排名前十榜单，云南下滑两个位次，江苏稳居首位，前三名的组成也无变化。

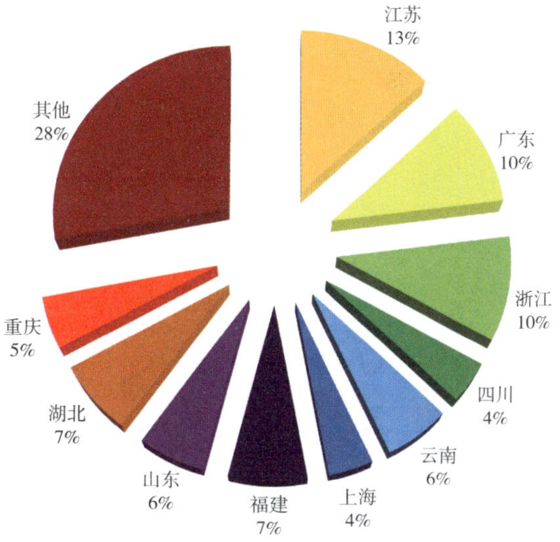

图3-6　2014年度接待国内旅游人次排名前十位的地区情况

二、出境旅游业务

2014年度全国旅行社出境旅游组织3914.98万人次、20911.77万人天，分别同比增长16.67%、24.74%。2014年，在国内经济社会发展良好基本面的支撑下，加上人民币升值、各国和各地区纷纷推出便利化政策等因素，我国出境旅游继续快速增长，但增长率呈回落态势。

图 3-7　2002～2014 年全国旅行社出境旅游组织人次数及增长率

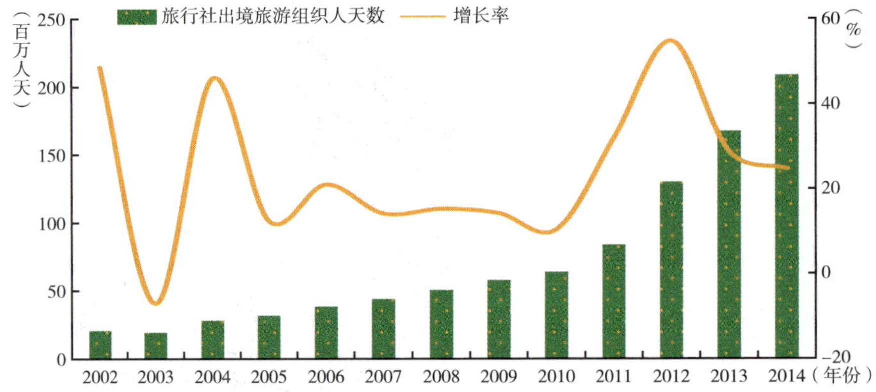

图 3-8　2002～2014 年全国旅行社出境旅游组织人天数及增长率

2014 年度旅行社出境旅游组织人次排名前十位的目的地国家和地区依次为中国香港、韩国、泰国、中国台湾、中国澳门、日本、新加坡、马来西亚、印度尼西亚、法国。

近年来，日本、韩国等都在以简化签证手续、购物优惠政策等吸引中国游客，2014 年，韩国超越泰国，居旅行社出境旅游组织人次排名第二位，日本提升两个位次，居第六位；中国香港仍居榜首，但其份额持续减少；印度尼西亚取代越南进入前十榜单。

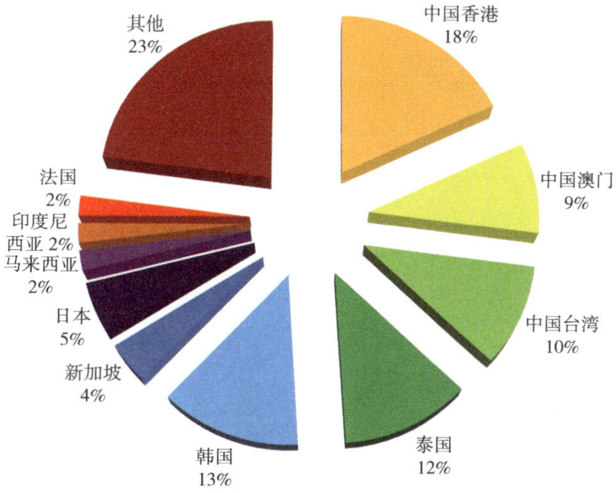

图 3-9　2014 年度组织出境旅游人次排名前十位的目的地国家或地区情况

三、入境旅游业务

2014 年度全国旅行社入境旅游外联 1410.04 万人次、6165.94 万人天，接待 2002.56 万人次、6855.15 万人天，分别同比减少 2.59%、增长 1.69%，减少 2.18% 和增长 2.81%。

2014 年，由于全球经济尚未完全复苏，我国旅游价格竞争力减弱，各国和各地

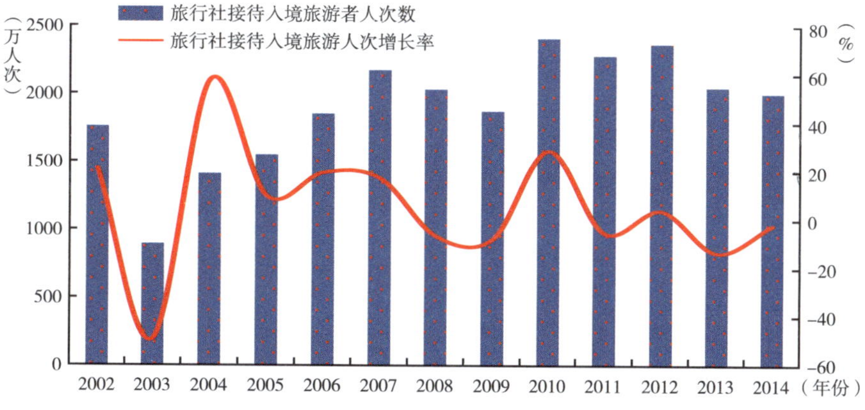

图 3-10　2002 ~ 2014 年全国旅行社接待入境旅游人次数及增长率

区加大了对旅游客源的争夺力度，而我国入境旅游发展进入成熟阶段，对当前国际旅游发展的新格局无法适应，加之雾霾、环境污染等多重因素的影响，入境旅游市场依然振兴乏力。

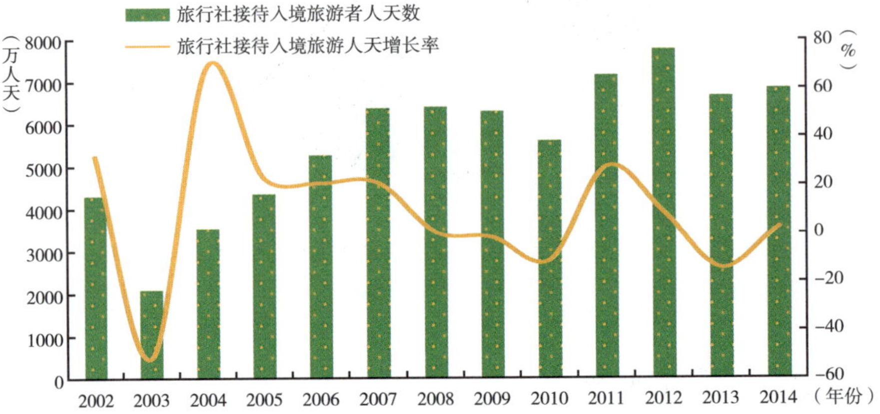

图 3-11　2002～2014 年全国旅行社接待入境旅游人天数及增长

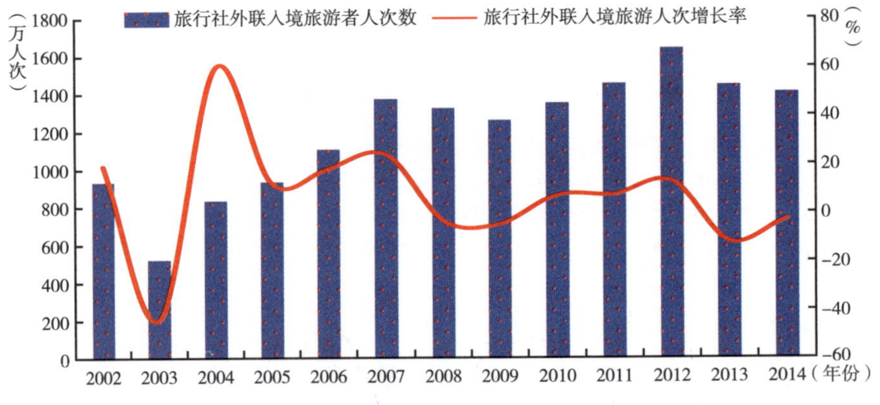

图 3-12　2002～2014 年全国旅行社外联入境旅游人次数及增长率

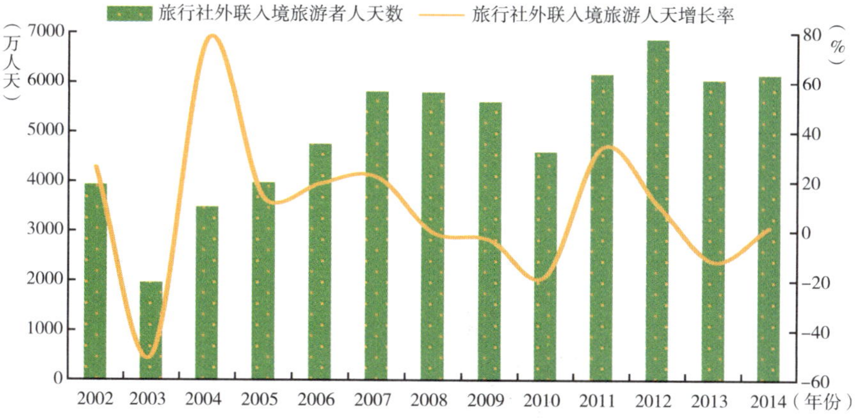

图 3-13　2002～2014 年全国旅行社外联入境旅游人天数及增长率

2014 年度旅行社入境旅游外联人次排名前十位的客源地国家和地区依次为中国香港、中国台湾、韩国、中国澳门、新加坡、美国、俄罗斯、日本、马来西亚、泰国。

2014 年，我国旅行社外联入境旅游的客源地国家或地区格局继续保持相对稳定。中国香港居首位，中国台湾与韩国互换位次分列第二位和第三位，中国澳门份额稍有上升，仍居第四位，新加坡上升一个位次，居第五位。

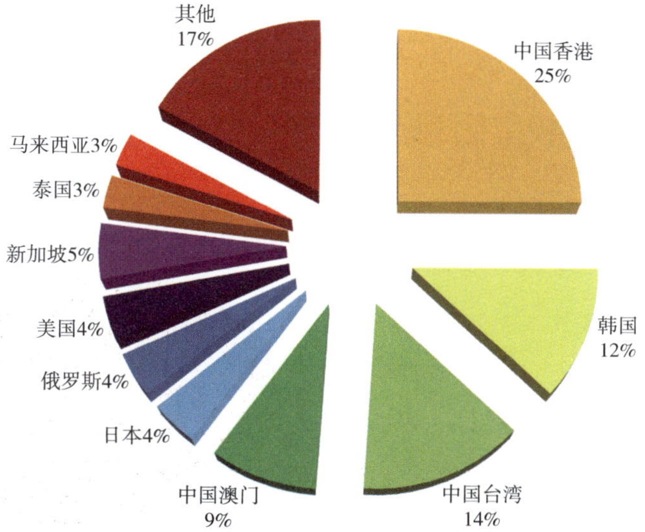

图 3-14　2014 年度外联入境旅游人次排名前十位的客源地国家或地区情况

2014 年度旅行社入境旅游接待人次排名前十位的客源地国家和地区依次为中国香港、中国台湾、韩国、中国澳门、美国、俄罗斯、新加坡、马来西亚、泰国、日本。

2014 年，我国旅行社接待入境旅游人次排名前六位的客源地国家或地区没有变化。我国港澳台份额均有上升，泰国份额下降 2 个百分点，下滑两个位次，新加坡上升两个位次，日本仍居榜尾。

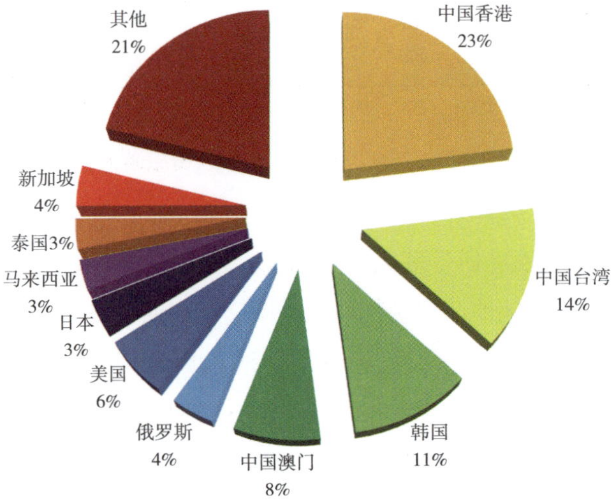

图 3–15　2014 年度接待入境旅游人次排名前十位的客源地国家或地区情况

四、分项业务情况比较

1. 2014 年度三大市场人次数比较

以入境旅游外联人次、国内旅游组织人次、出境旅游组织人次三项指标数据进行比较，2014 年度全国旅行社入境旅游、国内旅游、出境旅游所占份额分别为 8%、71%、21%，分别同比持平、减少 2 个百分点、增长 2 个百分点。

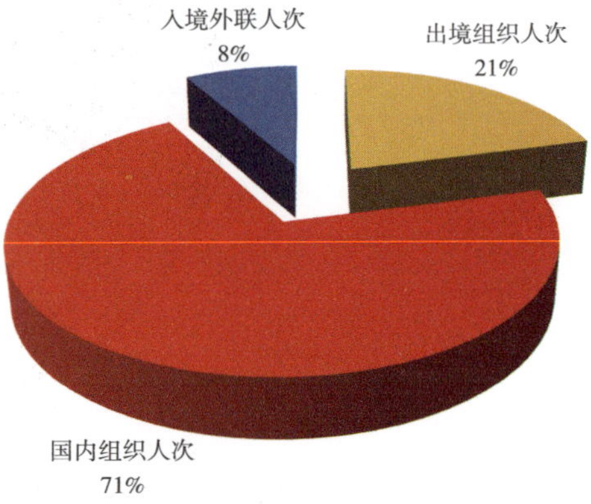

图 3–16　2014 年度三大旅游市场人次情况比较

2.2014 年度三大市场人天数比较

以入境外联人天、国内组织人天、出境组织人天三项指标数据进行比较，2014 年度全国旅行社入境旅游、国内旅游、出境旅游所占份额分别为 9%、61%、30%，分别同比减少 1 个百分点、减少 3 个百分点、增长 4 个百分点。

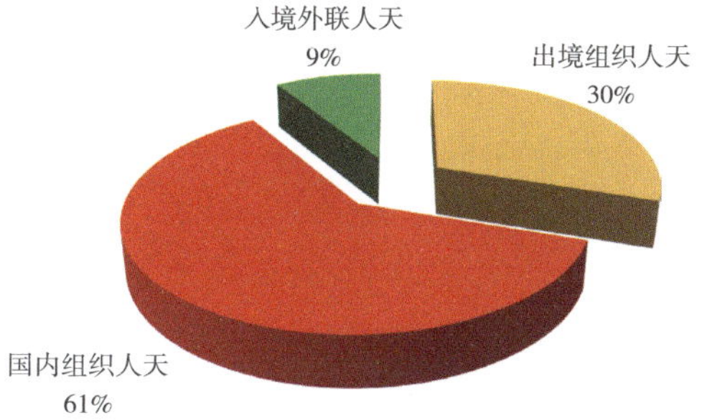

图 3–17　2014 年度三大旅游市场人天情况比较

3. 2014 年度三大市场营业收入比较

2014 年度全国旅行社国内旅游营业收入 1850.69 亿元，同比增长 5.03%，占全国旅行社旅游业务营业收入总量的 53.05%；国内旅游业务利润 91.91 亿元，同比增长 4.42%，占全国旅行社旅游业务利润总量的 53.35 %。

2014 年度全国旅行社出境旅游营业收入 1354.66 亿元，同比增长 17.07%，占全国旅行社旅游业务营业收入总量的 38.83%；出境旅游业务利润为 64.36 亿元，同比增长 8.23%，占全国旅行社旅游业务利润总量的 37.36 %。

2014 年度全国旅行社入境旅游营业收入 283.04 亿元，同比增长 4.77%，占全国旅行社旅游业务营业收入总量的 8.11%；入境旅游业务利润为 16.01 亿元，同比增长 8.17%，占全国旅行社旅游业务利润总量的 9.29 %。

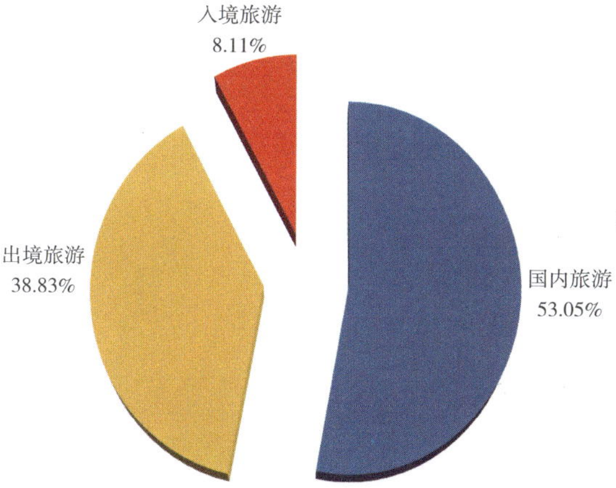

图 3–18　2014 年度三大旅游市场营业收入占全国比重情况比较

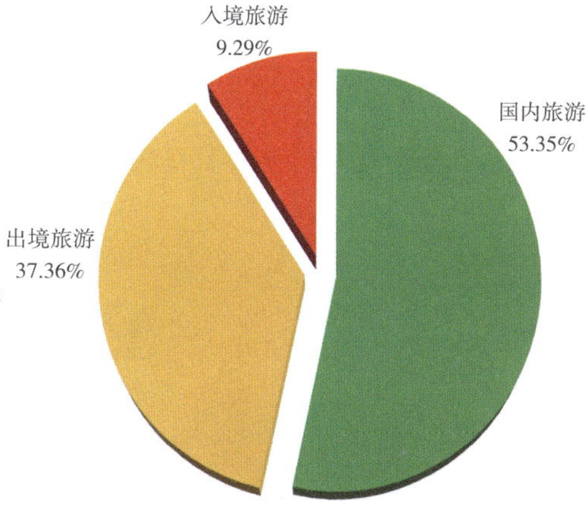

图 3–19　2014 年度三大旅游市场利润占全国比重情况比较

第四章

我国旅行社行业区域市场分析

一、华北地区行业分析（北京、天津、河北、山西和内蒙古）

1. 旅行社数量

2014 年，华北地区共有旅行社 4680 家，占全国旅行社总数的 17.56%。从数量分布上看，2014 年华北地区旅行社数量分布差异明显。其中，北京市、河北省的旅行社数量超过 1000 家，合计占比 56.52%；内蒙古、山西旅行社数量分别为 887 家

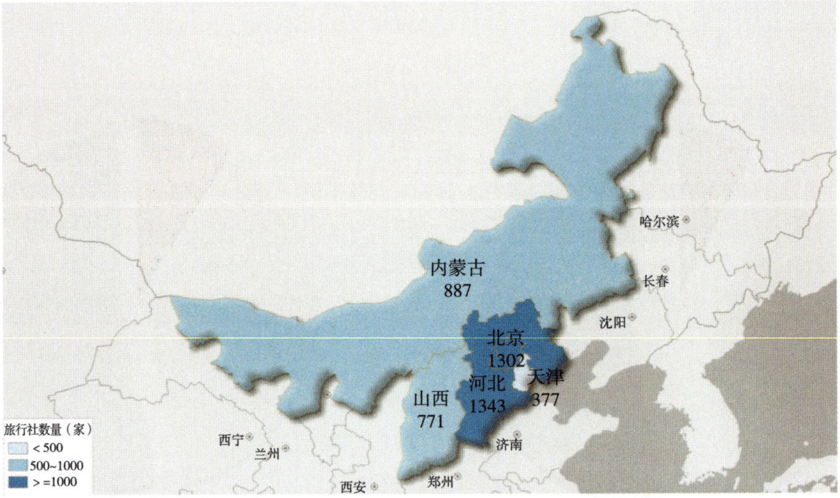

图 4–1　2014 年华北地区旅行社数量分布

地图来源：国家测绘局网站，审图号：GS（2014）6070 号

和 771 家，分别占比 18.95% 和 16.47%；值得关注的是，天津市旅行社数量最少，只有 377 家，占比 8.06%。

2. 旅游业务营业收入

2014 年度华北地区旅行社旅游业务营业收入 613.81 亿元，占全国旅行社旅游业务营业收入总数的 18.06%。从华北区域内各地区 2014 年营业收入看，北京独大，全年旅游业务营业收入为 481.30 亿元，占比 78.41%；山西、河北、天津全年实现旅游业务营业收入分别为 48.83 亿元、41.37 亿元和 24.98 亿元，合计占比 18.76%；内蒙古地区营业收入最少，只有 17.33 亿元，占比 2.82%。

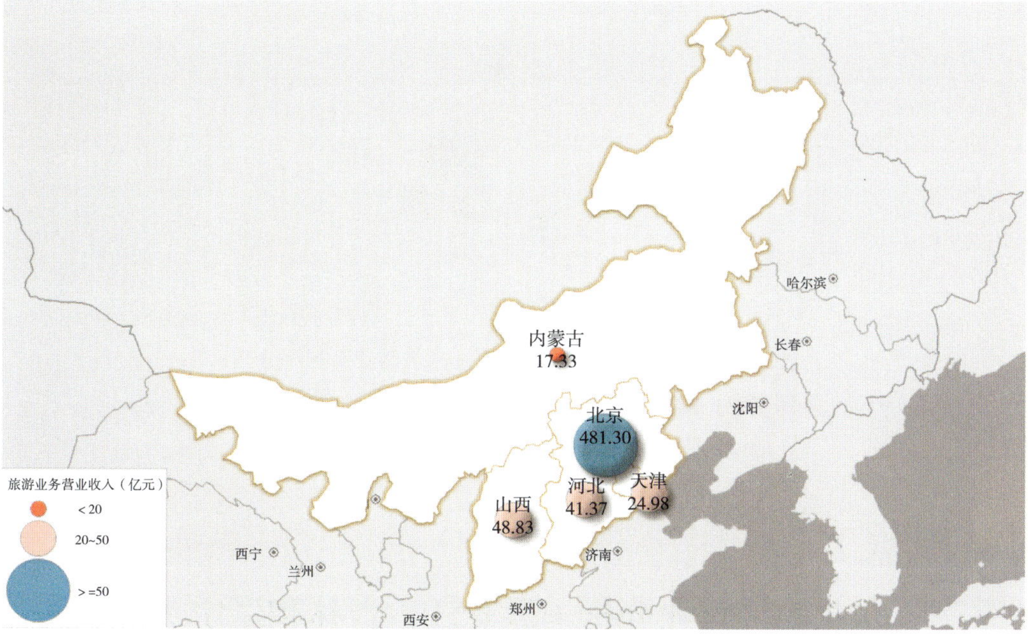

图 4-2　2014 年度华北地区旅行社旅游业务营业收入分布

地图来源：国家测绘局网站，审图号：GS（2014）6070 号

3. 旅游业务利润

2014 年度华北地区旅行社旅游业务利润 29.98 亿元，占全国旅行社旅游业务利润总数的 17.60%。在华北地区区域内旅游业务利润分布上，北京表现依然抢眼，全

年实现旅游业务利润 23 亿元，占比 76.72%；其次为河北省，全年旅游业务利润为 2.76 亿元，占比 9.21%；天津、山西、内蒙古均未达到 2 亿元，分别为 1.25 亿元、1.47 亿元和 1.50 亿元，合计占比 14.07%。

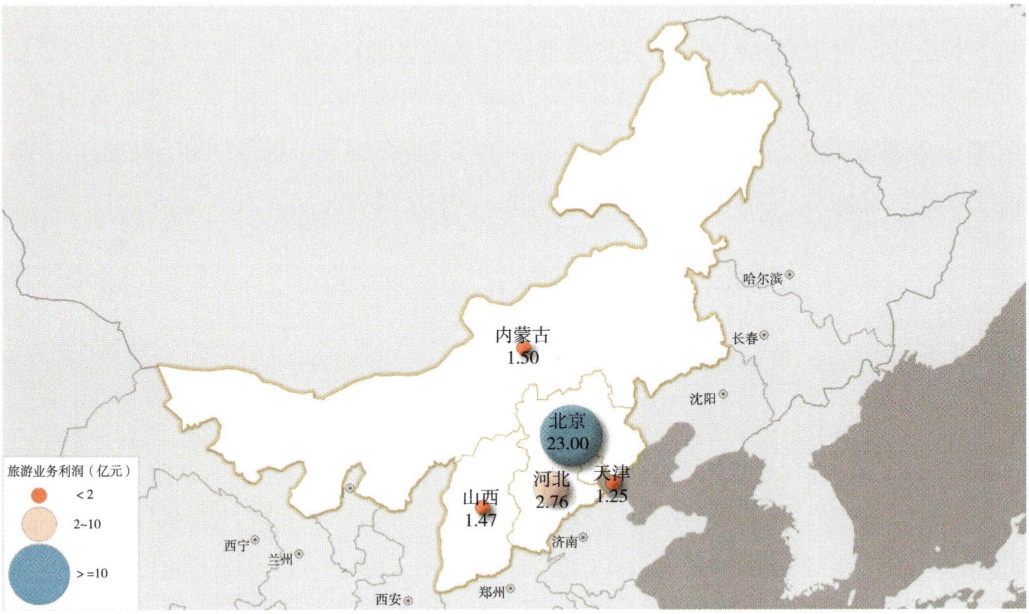

图 4-3　2014 年度华北地区旅行社旅游业务利润分布

地图来源：国家测绘局网站，审图号：GS（2014）6070 号

二、东北地区行业分析（黑龙江、吉林和辽宁）

1. 旅行社数量

2014 年，东北地区共有旅行社 2455 家，占全国旅行社总数的 9.21%。从东北地区区域内数量分布看，辽宁省占据半壁江山，旅行社数量为 1210 家，占比 49.29%；黑龙江次之，共有旅行社 663 家，占比 27%；吉林省数量最少，共有 582 家，占比 23.71%。

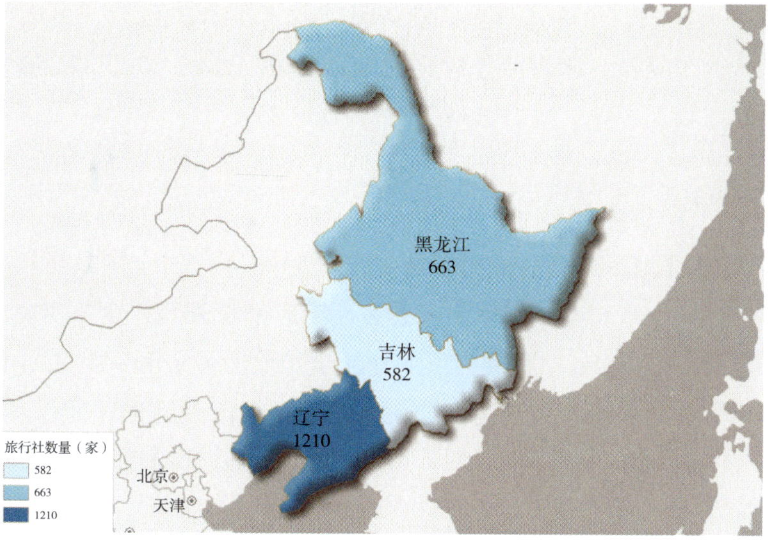

图 4-4　2014 年东北地区旅行社数量分布

地图来源：国家测绘局网站，审图号：GS（2014）6070 号

2. 旅游业务营业收入

2014 年度东北地区旅行社旅游业务营业收入 162.18 亿元，占全国旅行社旅游业务营业收入总数的 4.77%。从东北区域各地区 2014 年旅游业务营业收入占比看，

图 4-5　2014 年度东北地区旅行社旅游业务营业收入分布

地图来源：国家测绘局网站，审图号：GS（2014）6070 号

辽宁省表现最为强劲，全年实现旅游业务营业收入 111.25 亿元，占比 68.60%，接近七成；其次为黑龙江，旅游业务营业收入为 37.07 亿元，占比 22.85%；吉林省全年旅游业务营业收入最少，为 13.86 亿元，占比 8.55%。

3. 旅游业务利润

2014 年度东北地区旅行社旅游业务利润 8.54 亿元，占全国旅行社旅游业务利润总数的 5.01%。从东北地区区域内来看，辽宁省依然领跑，全年实现旅游业务利润 6.05 亿元，占比 70.84%；其次为黑龙江，全年旅游业务利润为 2.24 亿元，占比 26.23%；吉林省全年旅游业务利润仅有 0.25 亿元，占比不足 3%。

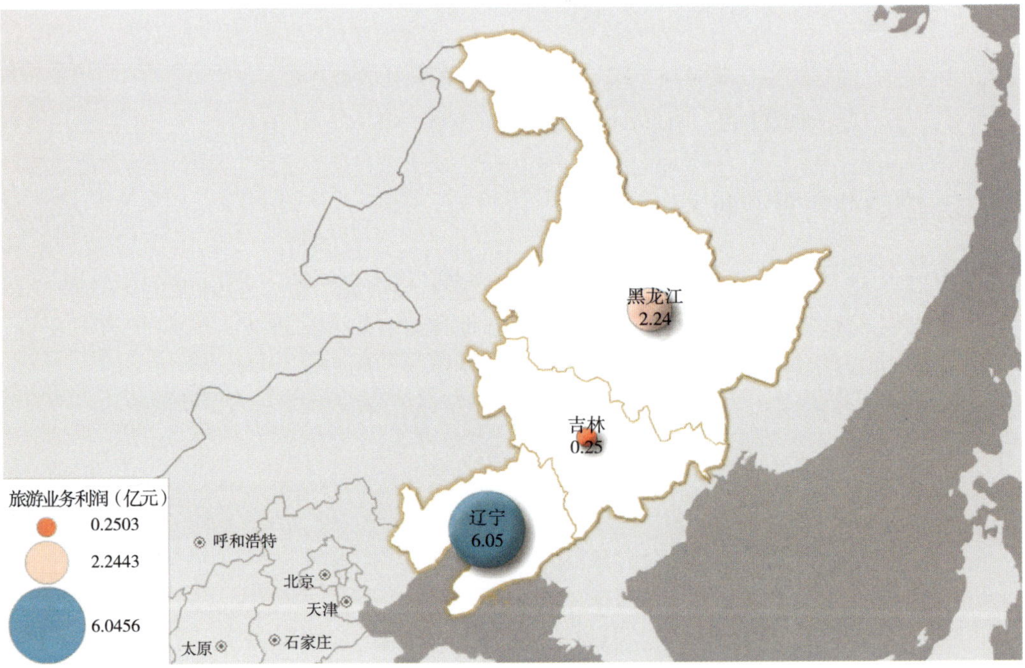

图 4-6　2014 年度东北地区旅行社旅游业务利润分布

地图来源：国家测绘局网站，审图号：GS（2014）6070 号

三、华东地区行业分析（山东、江苏、安徽、浙江、福建、江西和上海）

1. 旅行社数量

2014 年，华东地区共有旅行社 9976 家，占全国旅行社总数的 37.43%。从华东地区区域内分布看，山东、江苏、浙江三个省份旅行社数量超过 2000 家，分别为 2054 家、2099 家和 2036 家，合计占比 62.04%；上海、安徽两个省份旅行社数量超过 1000 家，分别为 1185 家和 1046 家，合计占比 22.36%；福建、江西两个省份旅行社数量不足 1000 家，分别为 805 家和 751 家，合计占比 15.60%。

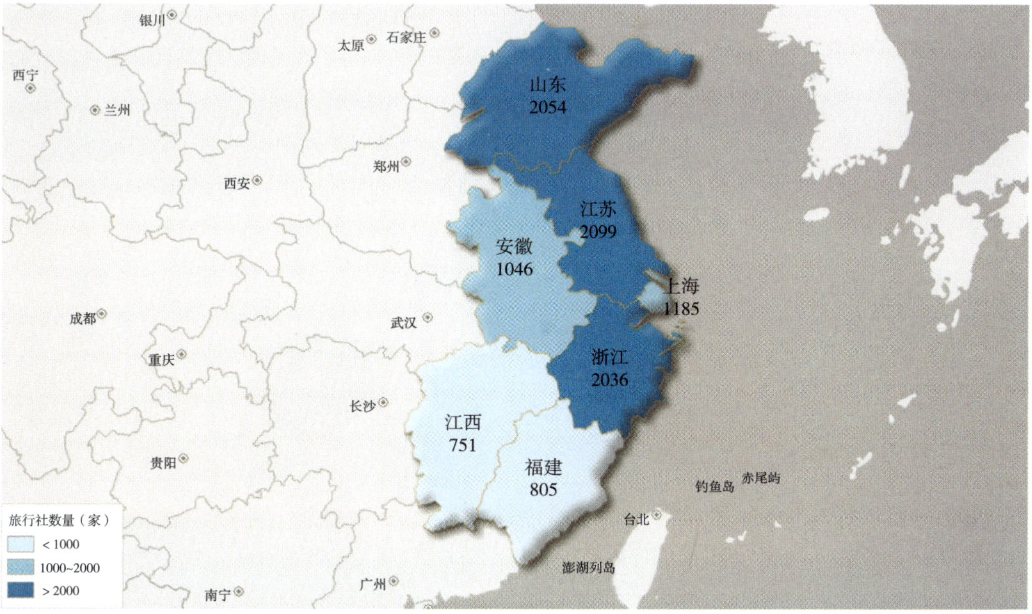

图 4-7　2014 年华东地区旅行社数量分布

地图来源：国家测绘局网站，审图号：GS（2014）6070 号

2. 旅游业务营业收入

2014 年度华东地区旅行社旅游业务营业收入 1353.90 亿元，占全国旅行社旅游业务营业收入总数的 39.84%。从华东地区区域内分布看，可分为四个梯队，第一梯队的上海全年实现旅游业务营业收入 510.22 亿元，占比 37.69%；第二梯队的江苏、浙江全年旅游业务营业收入超过 200 亿元，分别为 227.38 亿元和 224.17 亿元，合计占比 33.35%；第三梯队的山东、福建全年实现旅游业务营业收入 150 亿元以上，分别为 156.59 亿元和 150.99 亿元，合计占比 22.72%；第四梯队的安徽和江西两个省份全年旅游业务营业收入不足 100 亿元，分别为 52.37 亿元和 32.19 亿元，合计占比 6.25%。

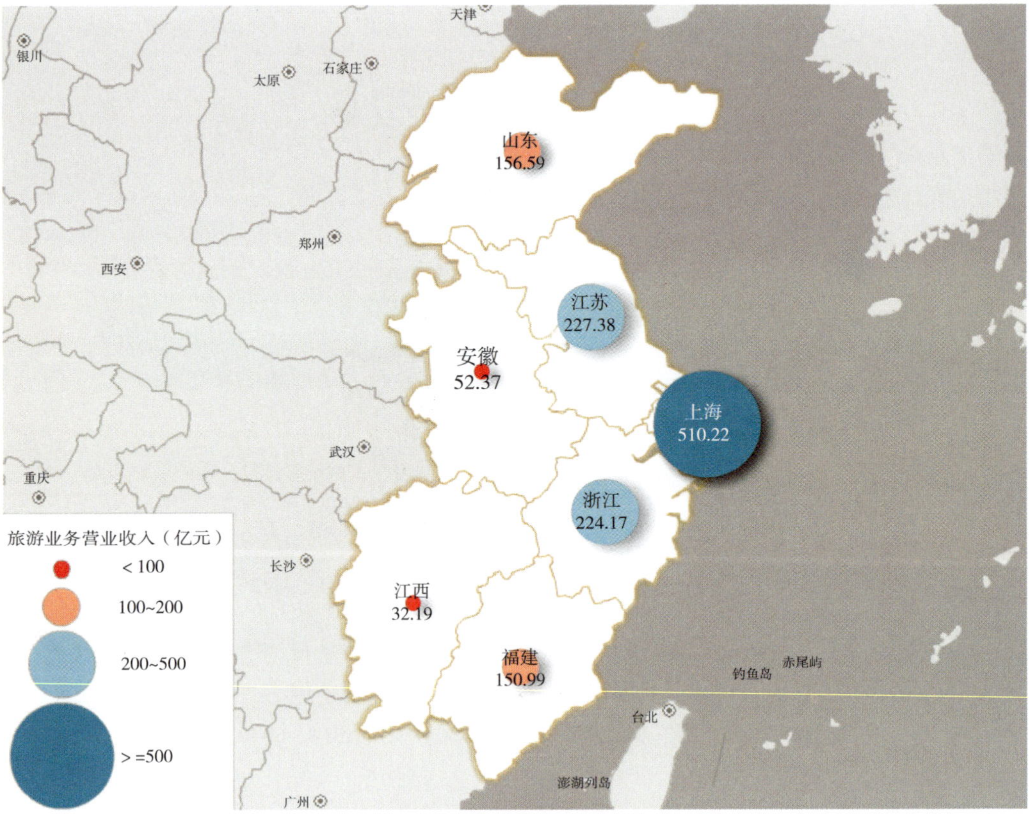

图 4-8　2014 年华东地区旅行社旅游业务营业收入分布

地图来源：国家测绘局网站，审图号：GS（2014）6070 号

3. 旅游业务利润

2014 年度华东地区旅行社旅游业务利润 64.05 亿元，占全国旅行社旅游业务利润总数的 37.60%。从地区上看，上海表现最为突出，全年实现旅行社旅游业务利润 19.19 亿元，占比 29.96%，接近三成；浙江、山东、江苏三个省份旅游业务利润超过 10 亿，分别为 11.14 亿元、10.56 亿元和 10.41 亿元，分别占比 17.39%、16.49% 和 16.25%；福建、安徽、江西三个省份全年旅游业务收入不足 10 亿元，分别为 7.70 亿元、3.48 亿元和 1.57 亿元，合计占比 19.91%。

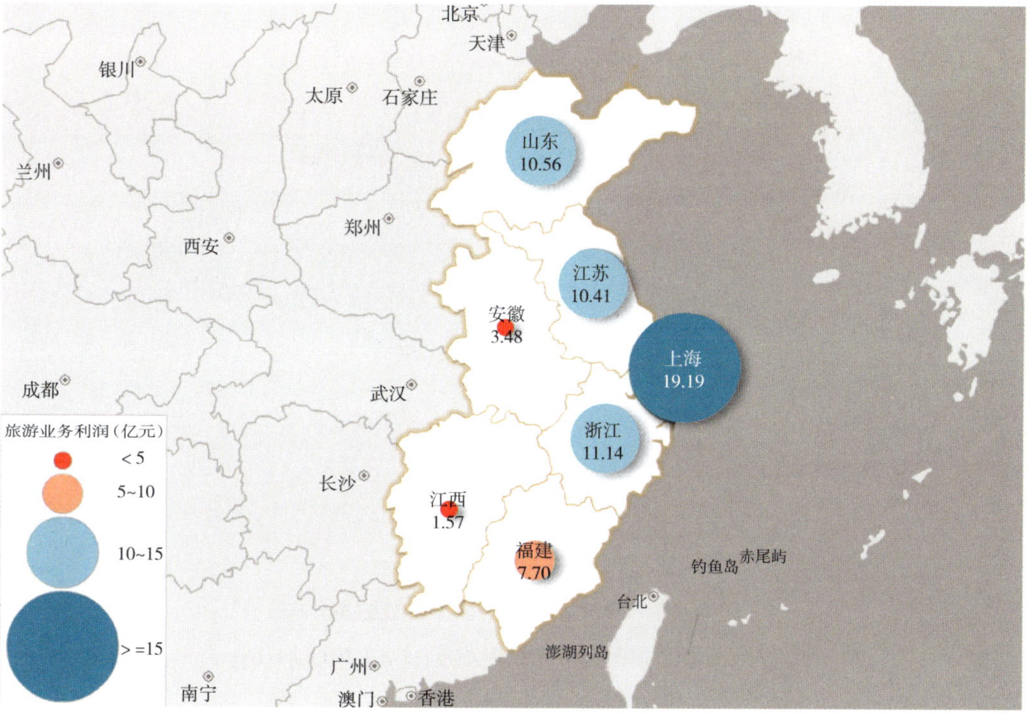

图 4–9　2014 年度华东地区旅行社旅游业务利润分布

地图来源：国家测绘局网站，审图号：GS（2014）6070 号

四、华南地区行业分析（广东、广西和海南）

1. 旅行社数量

2014 年，华南地区共有旅行社 2681 家，占全国旅行社总数的 10.06%。从数量分布看，华南地区呈现广东省一家独大的局面，拥有 1792 家旅行社，占比 66.84%；其次为广西，旅行社数量为 537 家，占比 20.03%；海南省拥有旅行社数量最少，为 352 家，占比 13.13%。

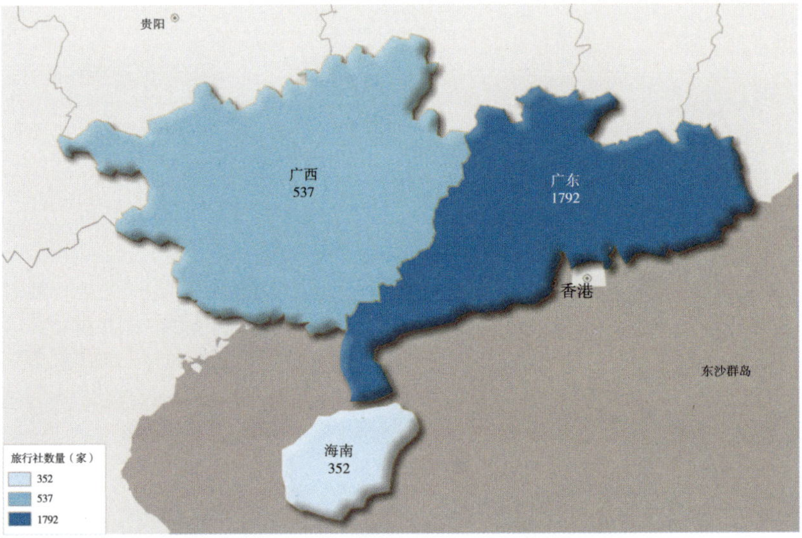

图 4–10　2014 年华南地区旅行社数量分布

地图来源：国家测绘局网站，审图号：GS（2014）6070 号

2. 旅游业务营业收入

2014 年度华南地区旅行社旅游业务营业收入 608.91 亿元，占全国旅行社旅游业务营业收入总数的 17.92%。从地区分布上看，广东省一家独大的局面在旅游业务营业收入指标上表现明显，广东省实现旅游业务营业收入 540.06 亿元，占比 88.69%；海南和广西全年实现旅游业务营业收入分别为 38.98 亿元和 29.88 亿元，合计占比 11.31%。

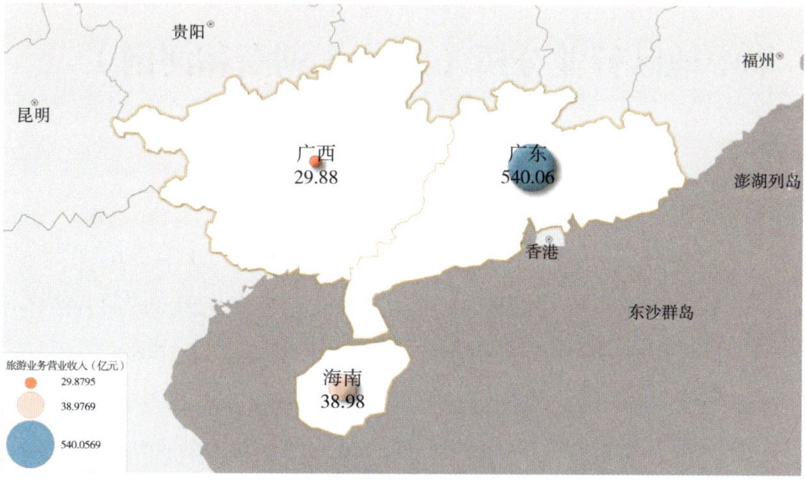

图 4–11 2014 年度华南地区旅行社旅游业务营业收入分布

地图来源：国家测绘局网站，审图号：GS（2014）6070 号

3. 旅游业务利润

2014 年度华南地区旅行社旅游业务利润 36.02 亿元，占全国旅行社旅游业务利润总数的 21.15%。从地区分布上看，广东省一家独大的局面在旅游业务营业收入指标上表现更为明显，广东省全年实现旅游业务利润 32.66 亿元，占比 90.67 %，超过九成；海南和广西旅游业务利润分别为 1.82 亿元和 1.55 亿元，合计占比 9.33%。

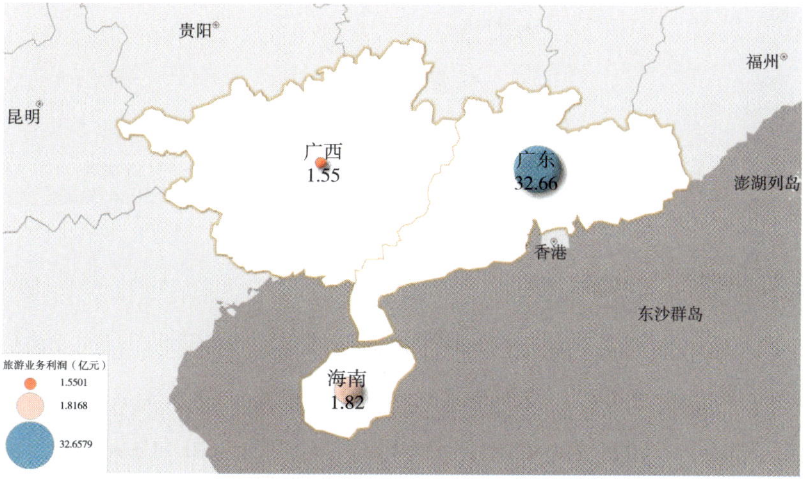

图 4–12 2014 年度华南地区旅行社旅游业务利润分布

地图来源：国家测绘局网站，审图号：GS（2014）6070 号

五、华中地区行业分析（湖北、湖南和河南）

1. 旅行社数量

2014 年，华中地区共有旅行社 2901 家，占全国旅行社总数的 10.89%。从数量分布看，河南、湖北两省 2014 年旅行社数量超过 1000 家，分别为 1100 家和 1050 家，占比 37.92% 和 36.19%；湖南省旅行社数量为 751 家，占比 25.89%。

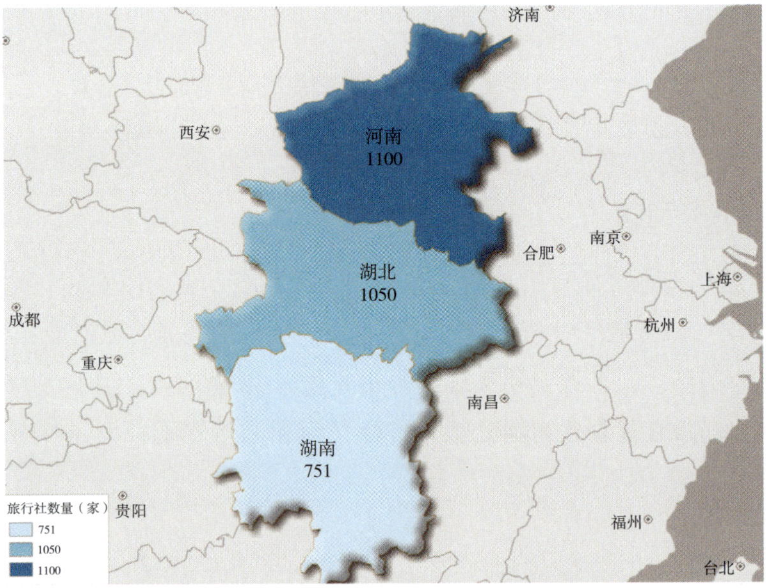

图 4-13　2014 年华中地区旅行社数量分布

地图来源：国家测绘局网站，审图号：GS（2014）6070 号

2. 旅游业务营业收入

2014 年度华中地区旅行社旅游业务营业收入 271.25 亿元，占全国旅行社旅游业务营业收入总数的 7.98%。从地区分布上看，湖北、湖南两省 2014 年全年旅行社旅游业务营业收入超过 100 亿元，分别为 118.24 亿元和 113.96 亿元，占比分别为 43.59% 和 42.01%；河南省全年旅游业务营业收入只有 39.05 亿元，占比仅为 14.40%。

图 4–14　2014 年度华中地区旅行社旅游业务营业收入分布

地图来源：国家测绘局网站，审图号：GS（2014）6070 号

3. 旅游业务利润

2014 年华中地区旅行社旅游业务利润 13.99 亿元，占全国旅行社旅游业务利润

图 4–15　2014 年度华中地区旅行社旅游业务利润分布

地图来源：国家测绘局网站，审图号：GS（2014）6070 号

总数的 8.21%。从地区分布上看，湖北、湖南两省全年旅游业务利润超过 5 亿元，分别为 6.61 亿元和 5.69 亿元，占比分别为 47.25% 和 40.67%；河南省全年实现旅游业务利润 1.69 亿元，占比仅为 12.08%。

六、西南地区行业分析（四川、云南、贵州、西藏和重庆）

1. 旅行社数量

2014 年，西南地区共有旅行社 2066 家，占全国旅行社总数的 7.75%。从西南地区区域内分布上看，云南、重庆两个省份的旅行社数量超过 500 家，分别为 704 家和 504 家，占比分别为 34.08% 和 24.39%；四川、贵州、西藏三个省份的旅行社数量不足 500 家，分别为 457 家、299 家和 102 家，合计占比 41.53%。

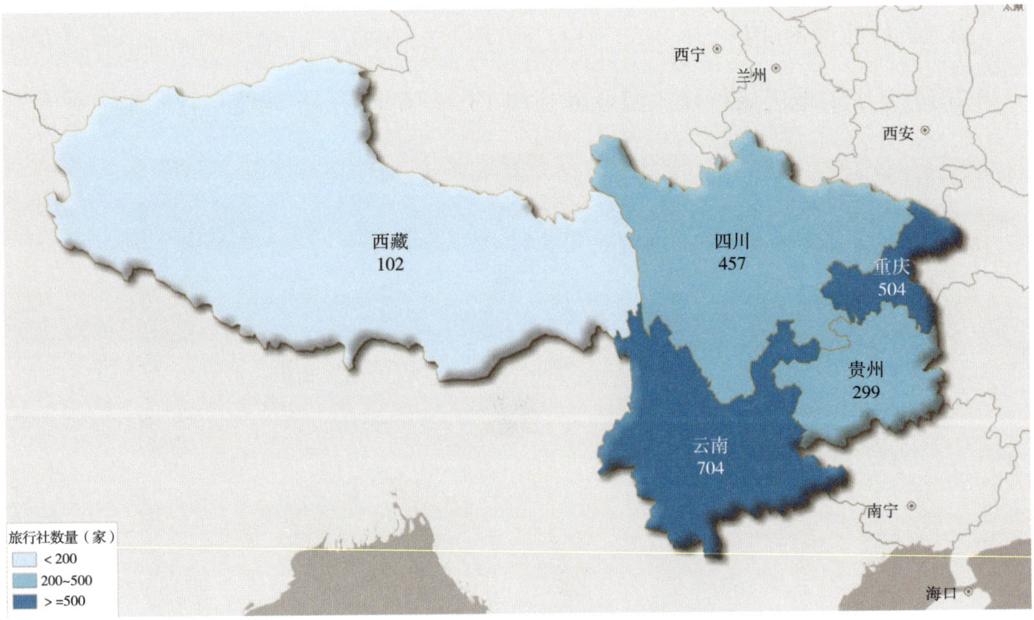

图 4-16　2014 年西南地区旅行社数量分布

地图来源：国家测绘局网站，审图号：GS（2014）6070 号

2. 旅游业务营业收入

2014 年度西南地区旅行社旅游业务营业收入 281.38 亿元，占全国旅行社旅游业务营业收入总数的 8.28%。2014 年度西南地区只有重庆市全年旅游业务营业收入超过 100 亿元，几乎占据了西南地区旅游业务营业总收入的半壁江山，全年实现旅游业务营业收入 122.78 亿元，占比 43.63%；云南、四川两个省份全年旅游业务营业收入分别为 89.99 亿元和 54.48 亿元，占比分别为 31.98%、19.36%；贵州和西藏全年旅游业务营业收入仅为 12.25 亿元和 1.87 亿元，分别占比 4.35% 和 0.66%。

图 4–17　2014 年度西南地区旅行社旅游业务营业收入分布

地图来源：国家测绘局网站，审图号：GS（2014）6070 号

3. 旅游业务利润

2014 年西南地区旅行社旅游业务利润 11.91 亿元，占全国旅行社旅游业务利润总数的 7.00%。从西南地区区域内分布来看，2014 年只有重庆旅游业务利润在 5 亿元以上，为 5.38 亿元，占比 45.17%；其次为云南省，全年旅游业务利润为 4.82 亿元，占比 40.47%；四川和贵州全年旅游业务利润分别为 1.31 亿元和 0.46 亿元，合计占比 14.86%；2014 年西藏地区全年旅游业务亏损 534.66 万元。

图 4-18　2014 年西南地区旅行社旅游业务利润分布

地图来源：国家测绘局网站，审图号：GS（2014）6070 号

七、西北地区行业分析（宁夏、新疆、青海、陕西和甘肃）

1. 旅行社数量

2014 年，西北地区（包括新疆生产建设兵团）共有旅行社 1891 家，占全国旅行社总数的 7.10%。2014 年西北地区旅行社数量唯一一个超过 500 家的省份是陕西省，有旅行社 687 家，占比 36.33%；甘肃、新疆、青海旅行社数量分别为 423 家、338 家和 237 家，合计占比 52.78%；宁夏地区和新疆生产建设兵团拥有旅行社数量为 114 家和 92 家，合计占比 10.89%。

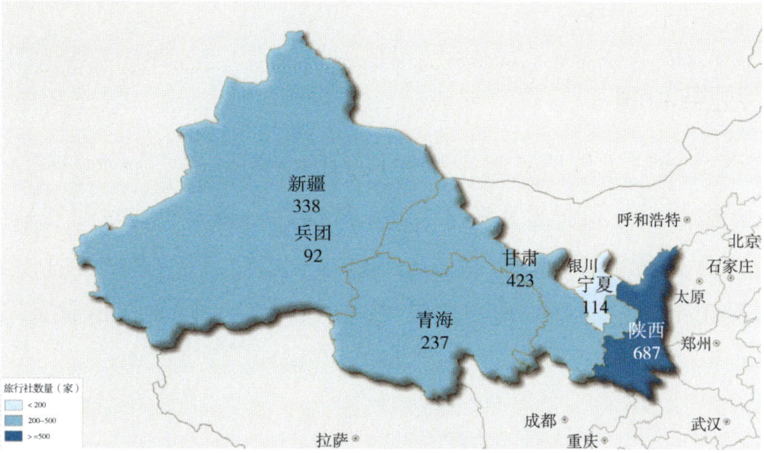

图 4-19　2014 年西北地区旅行社数量分布

地图来源：国家测绘局网站，审图号：GS（2014）6070 号

2. 旅游业务营业收入

2014 年度西北地区（包括新疆生产建设兵团）旅行社旅游业务营业收入 106.61 亿元，占全国旅行社旅游业务营业收入总数的 3.14%。从地区分布上看，陕西省领跑西北地区各省份，全年旅行社旅游业务营业收入 58.50 亿元，占比 54.87%；甘肃、新疆全年旅游业务营业收入分别为 16.04 亿元和 15.06 亿元，合计占比 29.17%；宁夏、新疆生产建设兵团和青海全年旅游业务营业收入分别为 6.07 亿元、5.59 亿元和

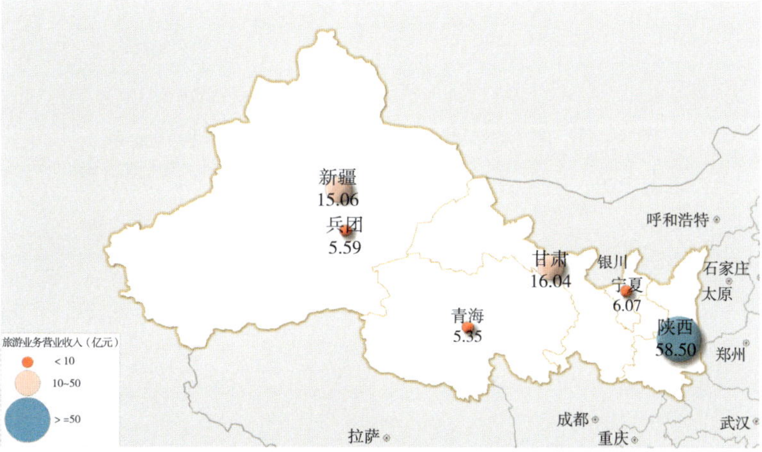

图 4-20　2014 年度西北地区旅行社旅游业务营业收入分布

地图来源：国家测绘局网站，审图号：GS（2014）6070 号

5.35 亿元，合计占比 15.96%。

3. 旅游业务利润

2014 年西北地区（包括新疆生产建设兵团）旅行社旅游业务利润 5.82 亿元，占全国旅行社旅游业务利润总数的 3.42%。从地区分布上看，陕西省依然领跑，全年实现旅游业务利润 3.94 亿元，占比 67.70%；其余新疆、青海、甘肃、宁夏、新疆生产建设兵团全年旅游业务利润均未超过 1 亿元，分别为 0.46 亿元、0.48 亿元、0.39 亿元、0.16 亿元和 0.37 亿元，合计占比 32.30%。

图 4-21　2014 年西北地区旅行社旅游业务利润分布

地图来源：国家测绘局网站，审图号：GS（2014）6070 号

Part Ⅱ

Research Report on the Development of Travel Agency in China (2015)

Chapter I

Current Situation of Travel Agency Industry Development in China

I. Review of Travel Agency Industry in 2014

1.1 The number of travel agencies grew, while the speed of growth slowed year by year

By the end of 2014, there are a total of 26650 travel agencies, with year-on-year growth of 2.29%. Since 2002, the total growth rate of Chinese travel agency shows a tendency of downward fluctuation. Since 2010, the year growth rate hovers around 5%, but it reached a lower record in 2014. But looked from aspects of the regions, the eastern provinces with developed economy and the Midwest provinces who especially attach great importance to the development of tourism still has a substantial increase. The province that had the highest growth in 2014 made the growth rate of 20%.

1.2 Travel agency assets grew, and the growth speed was rising

At the end of 2014, the Chinese travel agency assets totaled 129.297 billion yuan, up 24.35% from a year earlier. Among which, the debt is 84.812 billion yuan, up 21.65%, and the owners 'equity is 44.485 billion yuan, up 29.84%. Since 2011, the total travel agency assets grow rapidly, and the growth rate keeps rising, and more and more traditional travel agencies began to take the initiative to seek the integration development with capital market, meanwhile, the capital market also invested more enthusiasm into the industry.

1.3 Tourism business revenue grew, and the growth speed slightly rebounded

In 2014, the Chinese travel agency business revenue was 339.805 billion yuan, up 6.54% year-on-year, and which accounted for 84.33% of the whole revenue. 2014 was the second year after Tourism Law implementing, and the traditional travel agency industry kept innovating on the operation concept and the organization pattern, so as to adapt to market changes and the advent of the era of law. The group tourists become more and more satisfied with the tourism services provided by the travel agency. The annual travel revenue grew faster if compared with 2013.

1.4 Tourism business profit grew, and the growth speed kept declining

In 2014, the Chinese travel agency business profit was 17.032 billion yuan, up 4.96% year on year. Due to the factors, such as rising costs and market competition, although the total travel agency business profit kept rising, its growth speed declined for two consecutive years. Compared with 11.82% of 2012, it was down 6.86% in 2014.

1.5 Travel taxes grew, and the growth speed rose

In 2014, the true tax contributed by Chinese travel agencies was 2.416 billion yuan, up 8.00% year-on-year. From the historical data, the tax contributed by Chinese travel agencies presented high growth from 2004 to 2010, and it reached the highest record of 55.29% in 2010, while it slowed down after 2011. What is worthy paying attention is that compared with the increase rate (2.29%) of the tax contributed by Chinese travel agencies in the previous year, it grew 5.71% in 2014.

1.6 Travel agency employment was stable, and the proportion of highly educated employees kept rising

In 2014, the number of Chinese travel agency direct employees was 341,312, up 0.39%

from a year earlier. Among them, the number of employees with bachelor degrees or higher was 243,393, up 2.13% year-on-year. Since 2002, the increase speed of the number of Chinese travel agency employees keeps rising. Since 2010, the proportion of the number of employees who had college degrees or higher keeps increasing, rose from 61.63% in 2010 to 71.31% in 2014. The rate is near 10%.

II. Analysis of Travel Agency Market Characteristics in 2014

2.1 The extension of travel agency is in a historical stage of being expanded

With the rapid development of Internet, the online travel business instantly penetrates. The hotel and air tickets are firstly to be put online, and in addition, tourism vacation products, car rent services, scenic spot tickets and visa also accelerate their online process. These business operators have made the past tour service agencies those were not included in the category of travel agency start to enter the tourism service industry. The traditional travel agencies' business has been eroded by emerging industry, and the extension of travel agency is in a historical stage of being expanded.

2.2 Three main markets of travel agency show the phase characteristics of "two rising and one dropping"

In 2014, on the background of global economy recovering and domestic macro economy stabling, Chinese tourism economy resist downward pressure, and achieved "two rising and one dropping" in the tourism market. On the background of that domestic macro economy became stable and travel became more and more common for ordinary people, domestic tourism consumption demand maintain steady growth trend. As the global economy has not yet fully recovered from the financial crisis, China's tourism prices are less competitive. Because that other countries and regions pursue efforts to attract tourists,

Chinese tourism market enters the mature stage, and a wide range of haze weather and environment pollution, it is difficult for Chinese inbound tourism to recover. However, with the support of domestic economic and social development, combined with the appreciation of RMB, and other countries and regions have launched facilitation policies, Chinese outbound tourism continues to grow rapidly, and the growth rate falls back.

In 2014, the annual income of domestic tourism business was 178.368 billion yuan, up 1.22% from a year earlier, which accounted for 52.49% of the total tourism business revenue. In 2014, the annual income of outbound tourism business was 133.133 billion yuan, up 15.05% from a year earlier, accounting for 39.18% of the total tourism business revenue. In the same year, the annual income of inbound tourism business was 28.304 billion yuan, up 4.77% from a year earlier, accounting for 8.11% of the total tourism business revenue.

2.3 Capital markets push the traditional travel agency industry to transform and upgrade

Nowadays, in the historical stage of tourism industry competition, the capital has become the important competitive factor, and gradually become an important pushing force of business model innovation and construction, and boosts traditional industry upgrading. In 2014, UTS purchased Zhuyuan International Travel; Ctrip held the share of Yuanhua Travel with CITIC together; Yuniu purchased Classic Holiday and Zhongshan International Travel; Wonder Travel also stepped up its acquisitions – it purchased 12 offline traditional travel agencies in last year. The continued attention to capital market speed up traditional travel agency industry changing modes and adjusting structures, so that it can adapt to market changes better, and really appeal to meet the tourists' needs in the process of travel.

2.4 The domestic tourism market of travel agency has a steady rise, but the proportion decreases

As the tourism consumers increasingly become mature, their habits change, the number of private cars increases and roads develop rapidly, the individual market quickly grows, and the market of group travel depending agencies keeps shrinking. From 2009 to 2009, the proportion of domestic tourists of domestic group tour declines in all of the domestic tourists, the percentages of 5 years respectively are 5.31%, 5.71%, 5.19%, 4.87% and 5.31%. In the first half of 2014, all of the Chinese travel agencies organized 18.7391 million tourists to travel in China, which accounted for only 2.8%. The position of the tour market of group travel in domestic tourism market continues to decline.

2.5 Large regional imbalance exists in travel agency industry

Both in terms of number of travel agencies and the indicators of the travel agency business, large regional imbalance exist in the whole travel agency industry. Among all the regions, the east China area has the most eye-catching performance; the followings are north and south China; the developments of northwest, southwest and northeast areas relatively lag behind. From the aspect of the number of travel agencies, it accounted for 37.43% in east China in 2014 of the total amount in China; it accounted for 17.56% in north China; while they accounted for respectively 7.75% and 7.10% of northwest and southwest regions. From the index of travel agency tourism income, it accounted for 39.84% in east China in 2014 of the total amount in China; it accounted for 18.06% in north China; while they accounted for respectively 3.14% and 4.78% of northwest and southwest regions, totally accounted for less than 10%.

Chapter II

The Scale and Business Situation of Chinese Travel Agency Industry

I. The Number and Scale of Travel Agencies

1.1 The number of travel agencies

By the end of 2014, the total number of travel agencies is 26650, up 2.29% year-on-year. From the aspects of the growth of the provinces (municipalities and autonomous regions), the number of travel agencies in 10 provinces such as Sichuan, Hunan and Henan decreased, and Sichuan has the biggest decline of 22.01%; the numbers of that of Chongqing, Hainan, Tibet and Xinjiang Production and Construction Corps were the same; the numbers of travel agencies in the rest 18 provinces had varying degrees of growth, and Ningxia had the biggest increase of 20%; moreover, Yunnan and Beijing had the increase more than 10%.

With the rise of mass tourism and the unceasing reform of holiday system, people have more and more demand for tourism services. Since 2002, the total number of travel agencies has in a state of increase. But as a result of technological advances and mass consumption pattern changes, the development space of traditional travel agency industry is constantly extruded. Its growth rate shows a tendency of downward fluctuations in recent years, and since 2010, the year growth rate hovers around 5%, and it reached a new low record in 2014.

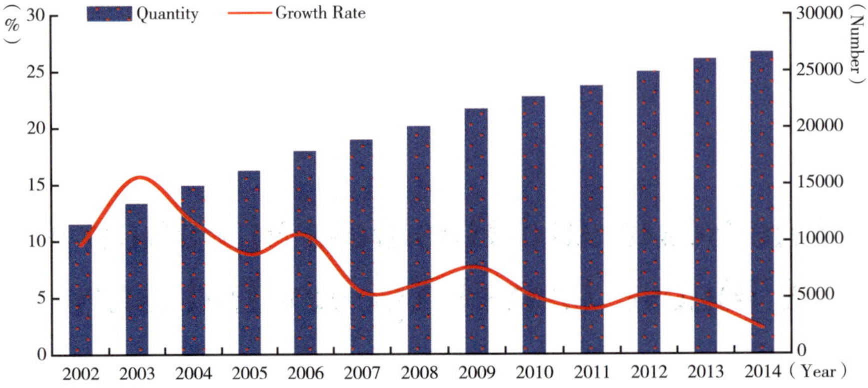

Graph 2-1 The number of Chinese travel agencies in 2002-2014

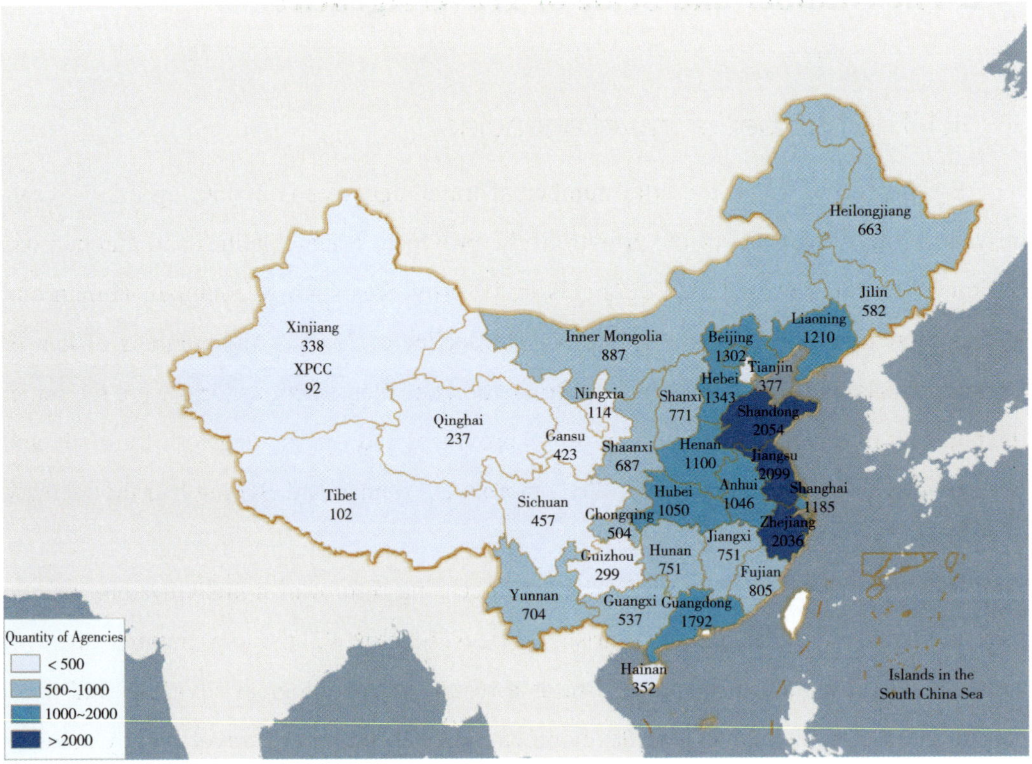

Graph 2-2 Distribution of travel agencies in each area in 2014

地图来源：国家测绘局网站，审图号：GS（2014）6070 号

1.2 The scale of Chinese travel agency assets

The Chinese travel agency assets are 129.297 billion yuan, up 24.35% from a year earlier; among which, the debt is 84.812 billion yuan, up 21.65% from a year earlier; and the owners' equity is 44.485 billion yuan, up 29.84% from a year earlier. Since 2002, the total travel agency assets showed a trend of fluctuations in growth, and a few drops were brought by force majeure, for example SARS in the first half of 2003, bird flu in 2005, and the global financial crisis in 2008. In addition to this, the total assets increased in the rest of the year. After the rapid growth in 2009 and 2010, it fell back slightly in 2011. After 2011, the total assets of Chinese travel agencies grew fast, and the growth rate kept in high level. In 2014, “the first private travel agency” - UTS Travel had several limits after IPO, and China CYTS Tours and CITS also became popular in capital market. More and more traditional travel agencies began to seek integrative development with capital market, actively responded to the challenges.

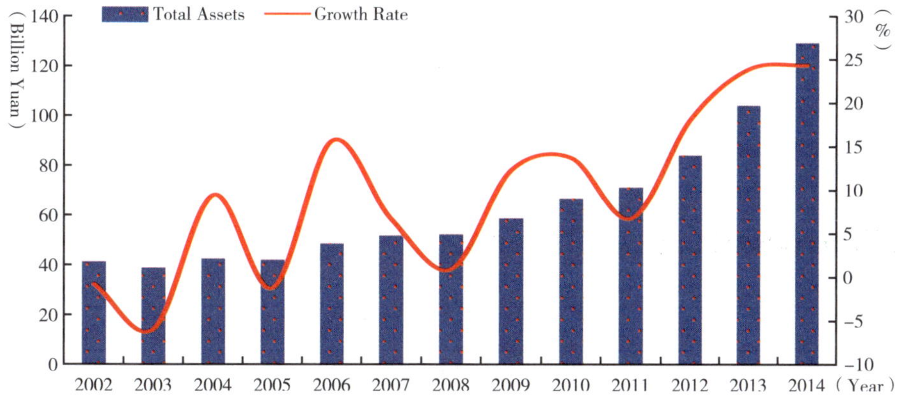

Graph 2-3 Total assets of Chinese travel agencies in 2002-2014

1.3 The percentage of the number of travel agencies in seven main areas in China

In 2014, there were 4680 travel agencies in north China, accounting for 17.56% of the total number; there were 2455 travel agencies in northeast China, accounting for 9.21% of the total number; there were 9976 travel agencies in east China, accounting for 37.43% of the total number; there were 2681 travel agencies in south China, accounting for 10.06% of the total number; there were 2901 travel agencies in central China, accounting for 10.89% of the total number; and there were 1891 travel agencies in northwest China (including Xinjiang Production and Construction Corps), accounting for 7.10% of the total number.

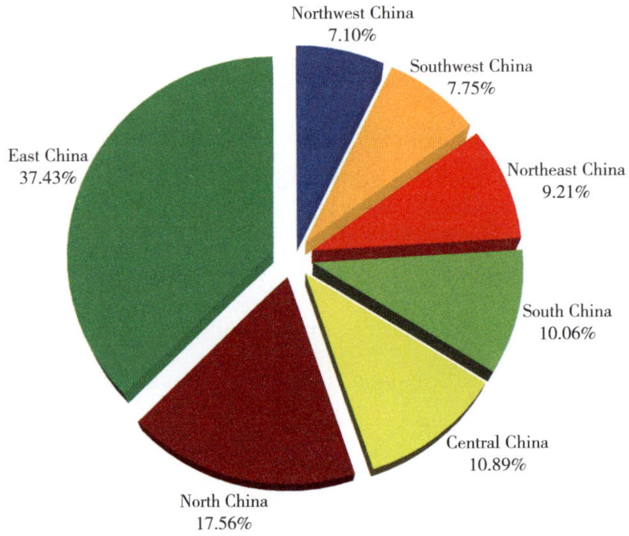

Graph 2-4 The percentage of the number of travel agencies in seven main areas in China in 2014

II. Tourism Business Revenue

2.1 Chinese tourism business revenue

In 2014, the tourism business revenue was 339.805 billion yuan, up 6.54% from a year earlier, accounting for 84.33% of the total revenue. From 2002 to 2010, except for the special years, such as 2003, 2005 and 2008, Chinese tourism business revenue kept in growth. Because of the existence of these special years, the growth rate of tourism business revenue presented a volatile state. Since 2010, influenced by bad economic environment, a lot of industries were implicated, and the growth speed of tourism business revenue was in a downward trend of fluctuations.

2014 is the second year after implementation of Tourism Law, development and management of tourism followed by the law made important progress. Through perfecting tourism management and governing market order, group tourists became more and more satisfied to the services provided by the travel agencies, and made a new high record. Traditional tourism industry is trying to innovation on operation concept and organization pattern, so as to adapt to market changes and welcome the era of law coming. The tourism business revenue in the whole year grew faster compared with 2013.

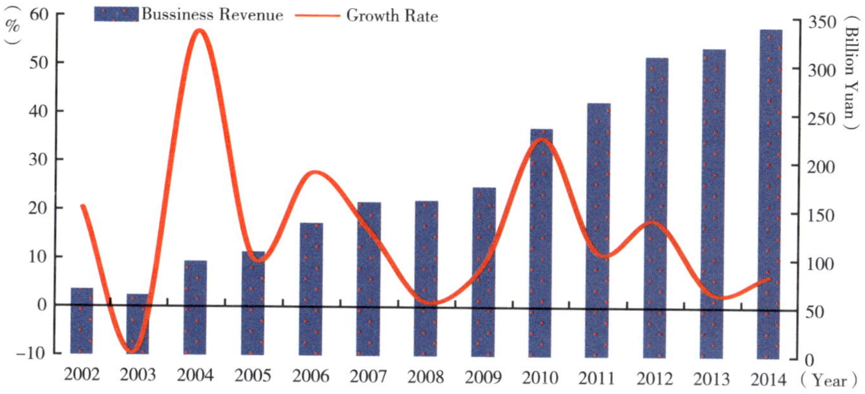

Graph 2-5 Total Chinese tourism business revenue in 2002-2014

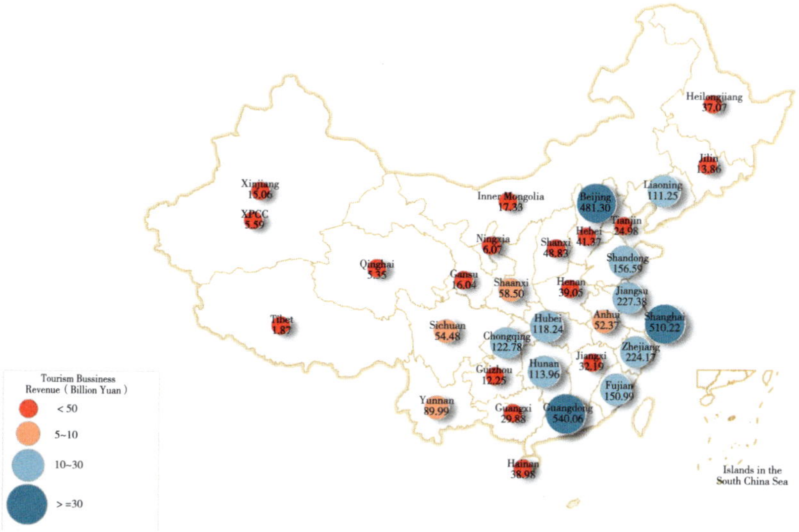

Graph 2-6 Distribution of tourism business revenue in each area of China in 2014

地图来源：国家测绘局网站，审图号：GS（2014）6070 号

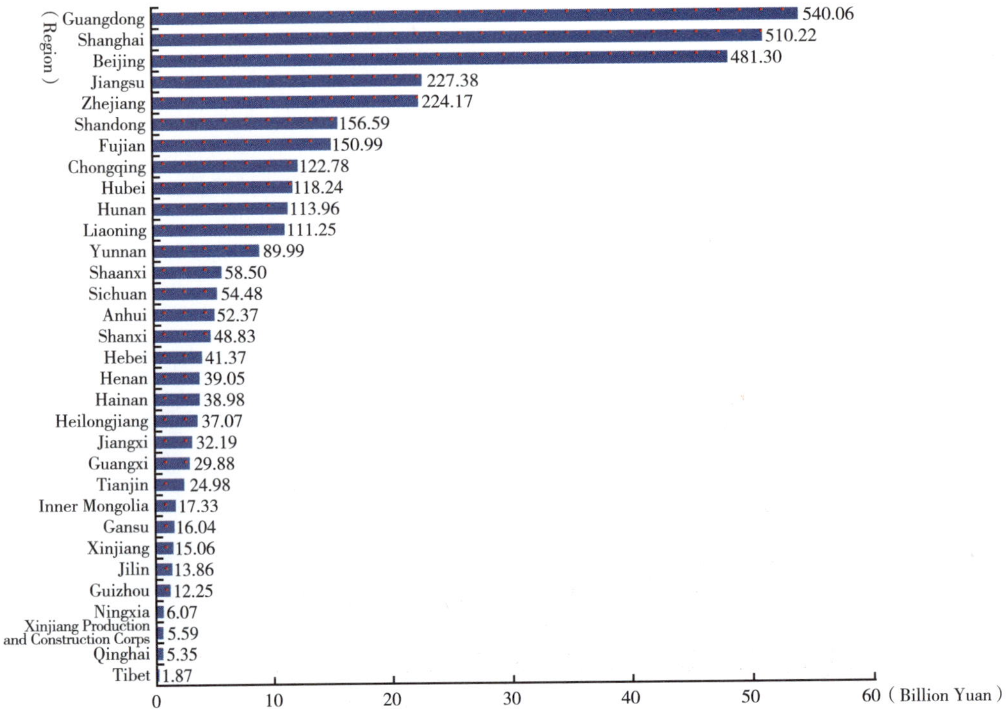

Graph 2-7 Tourism business revenue in each area of China in 2014

2.2 Distribution of tourism business revenue in the seven main regions

In 2014, the tourism business revenue in north China was 61.381 billion yuan, accounting for 18.06% of the total tourism business revenue in China; the tourism business revenue in northeast China was 16.218 billion yuan, accounting for 4.77%; the tourism business revenue in east China was 135.39 billion yuan, accounting for 39.84%; the tourism business revenue in south China was 60.891 billion yuan, accounting for 17.92%; the tourism business revenue in central China was 27.125 billion yuan, accounting for 7.98%; the tourism business revenue in southwest China was 28.138 billion yuan, accounting for 8.28%; and the tourism business revenue in northwest China (including Xinjiang Production and Construction Corps) was 10.661 billion yuan, accounting for 3.14%.

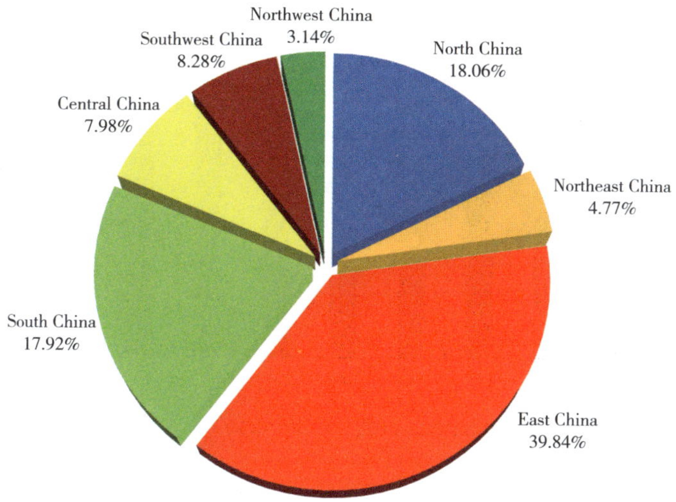

Graph 2-8 Distribution of tourism business revenue in the seven main regions in 2014

III. Tourism Business Profit

3.1 Tourism business profit of Chinese travel agencies

In 2014, the tourism business profit of Chinese travel agencies was 17.032 billion yuan, up 4.96% from a year earlier. Since 2004, the tourism business profit is in a rising trend, but its growth rate has been in a state of decline, except in the special years, such as 2005 and 2008. It was slight higher in 2011 than in 2010. Since 2012, due to the factors such as rising costs and market competition, the tourism business profit of Chinese travel agencies presents a new round of declining. In 2014, the profit grew slowly and the growth speed was in the lowest level in nearly three years.

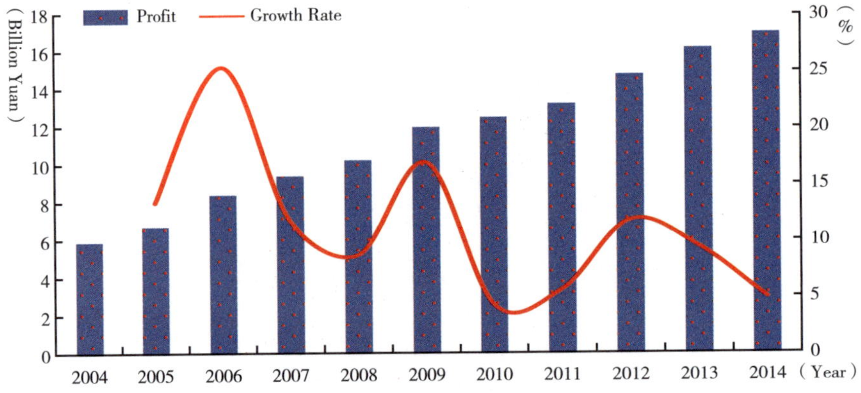

Graph 2–9 Total tourism business profit of Chinese travel agencies in 2004–2014

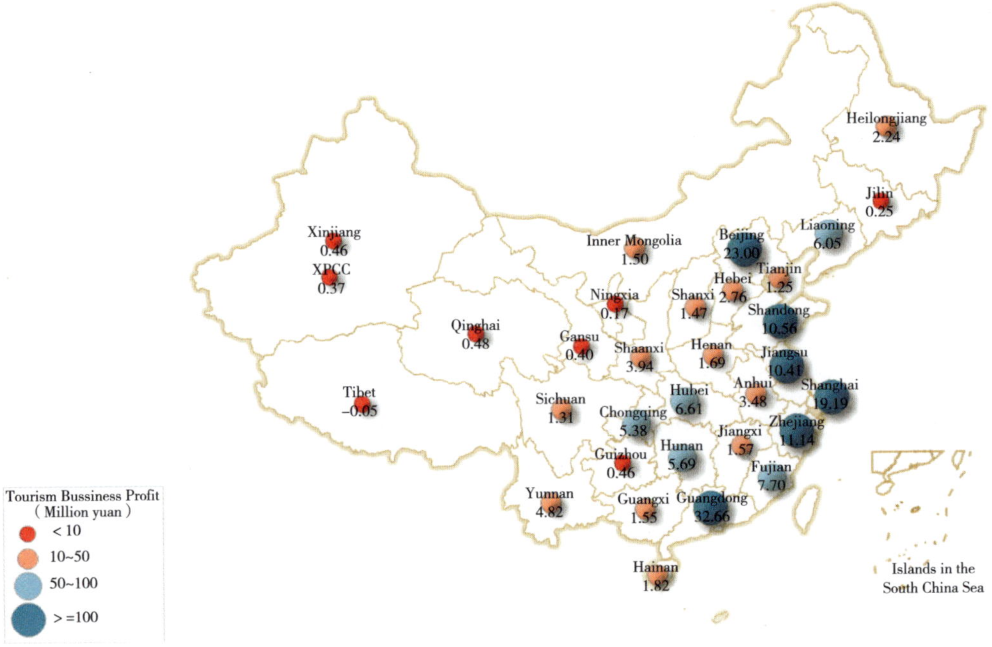

Graph 2–10 Distribution of total tourism business profit of Chinese travel agencies in 2014

地图来源：国家测绘局网站，审图号：GS（2014）6070 号

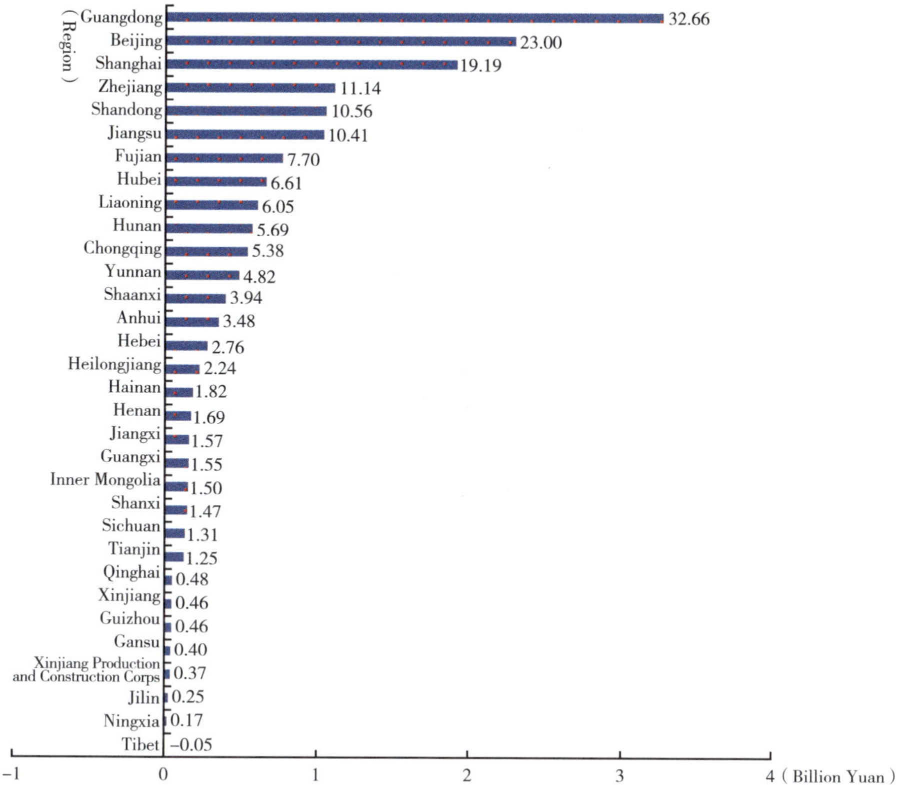

Graph 2–11 Total tourism business profit of Chinese travel agencies in 2014

3.2 Distribution of tourism business profit in seven main regions

In 2014, the tourism business profit in north China was 2.998 billion yuan, accounting for 17.60% of the total tourism business profit of Chinese travel agencies; the tourism business profit in northeast China was 854 million yuan, accounting for 5.01%; the tourism business profit in east China was 6.405 billion yuan, accounting for 37.60%; the tourism business profit in south China was 3.602 billion yuan, accounting for 21.15%; the tourism business profit in central China was 1.399 billion yuan, accounting for 8.21%; the tourism business profit in southwest China was 1.191 billion yuan, accounting for 7.00%; and the tourism business profit in northwest China (including Xinjiang Production and Construction Corps) was 582 million yuan, accounting for 3.42%.

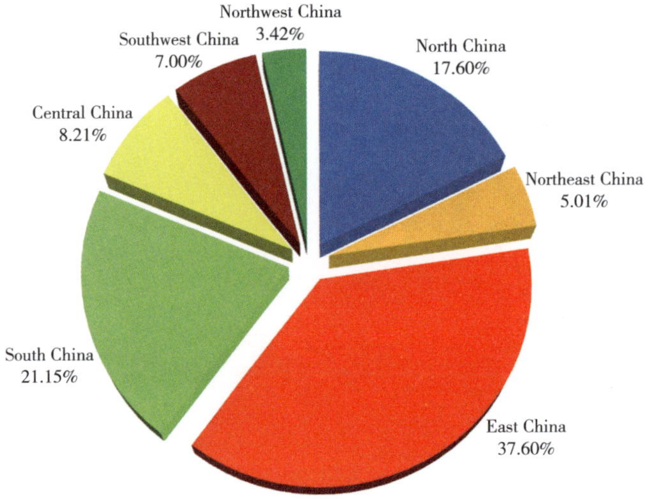

Graph 2-12 Distribution of tourism business profit in seven main regions in 2014

IV. Paid-in Tax

4.1 The paid-in tax of Chinese travel agencies

In 2014, the paid-in tax of Chinese travel agencies was 2.416 billion yuan, up 8.00% from the earlier year. The amount of paid-in tax of travel agencies and the fluctuations of growth rate are closely linked to the operating revenue and profit of the travel agencies, and the overall situation is quite similar. From past years it can be seen that, since 2004, the paid-in tax of travel agencies was in a high growth trend, although in the special year of 2005, it also reached 16.82%, and achieved a growth of 2.89% in 2008.

The growth rate of paid-in tax of travel agencies reached the highest level in 2010, and shrank sharply in 2011. It became slower and slower in the following years.

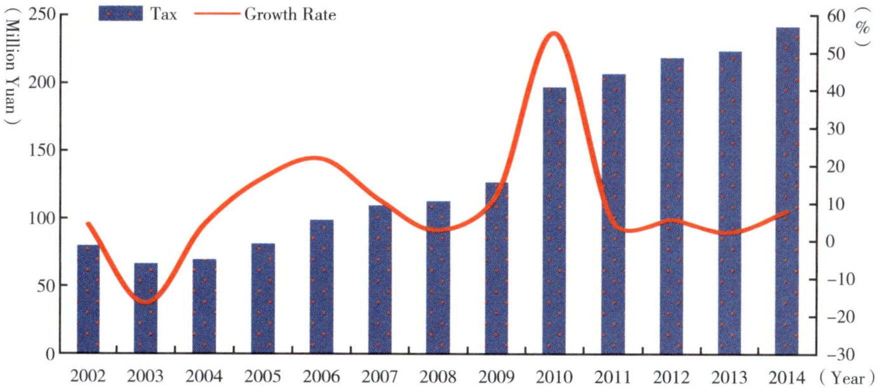

Graph 2-13 The paid-in tax of Chinese travel agencies in 2002-2014

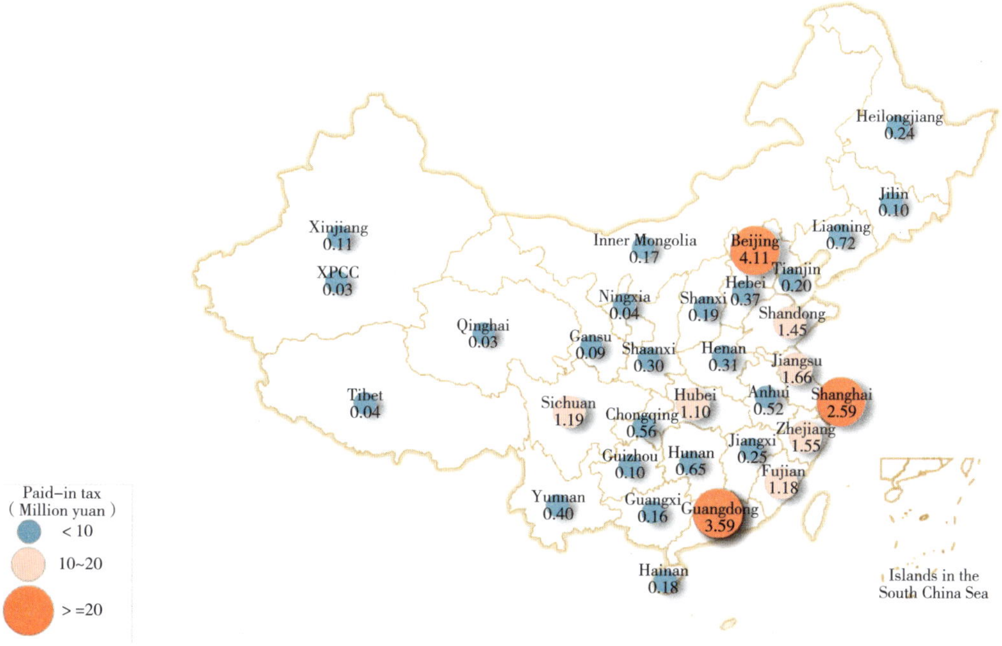

Graph 2-14 Distribution of paid-in tax of Chinese travel agencies in 2014

地图来源：国家测绘局网站，审图号：GS（2014）6070 号

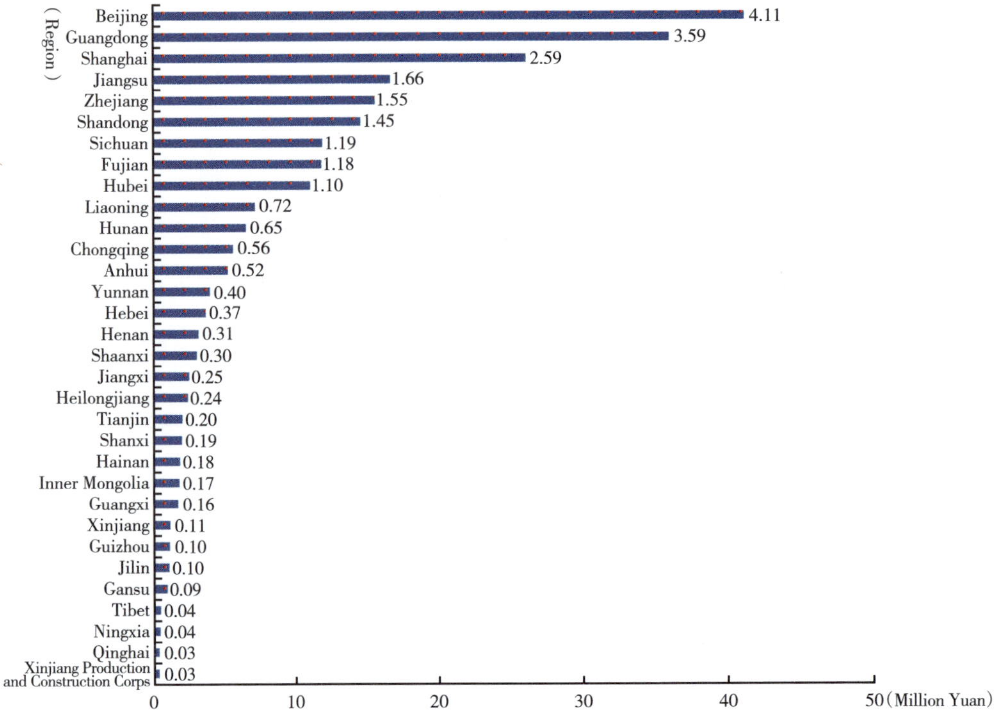

Graph 2-15 The paid-in tax of Chinese travel agencies in 2014

4.2 Distribution of paid-in tax in seven main regions

In 2014, the paid-in tax of travel agencies in north China was 504 million yuan, accounting for 20.84% of the total paid-in tax of Chinese travel agencies; the paid-in tax in northeast China was 105 million yuan, accounting for 4.35%; the paid-in tax in east China was 921 million yuan, accounting for 38.12%; the paid-in tax in south China was 393 million yuan, accounting for 16.26%; the paid-in tax in central China was 207 million yuan, accounting for 8.55%; the paid-in tax in southwest China was 229 million yuan, accounting for 9.46%; and the paid-in tax in northwest China was 59 million yuan, accounting for 2.42%.

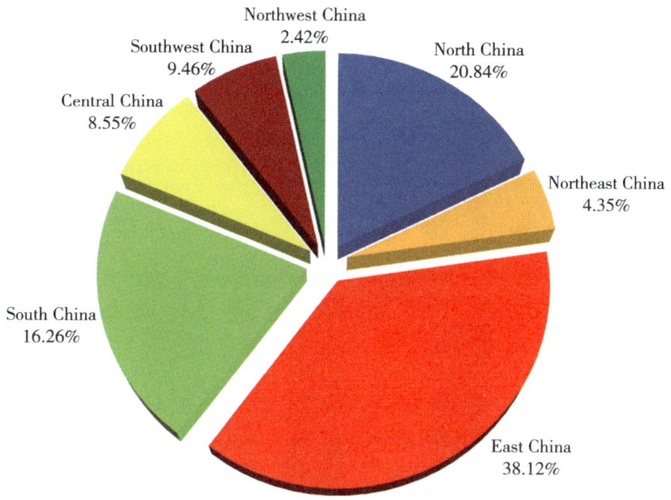

Graph 2-16 Distribution of paid-in tax in seven regions in 2014

V. Human Resource

In 2014, the number of employees of travel agencies was 341312, up 0.39% year-on-year. Among them, the number of employees with college or higher degrees was 243393, up 2.13% year-on-year. It is notable that, since 2010, the percentage of employees with

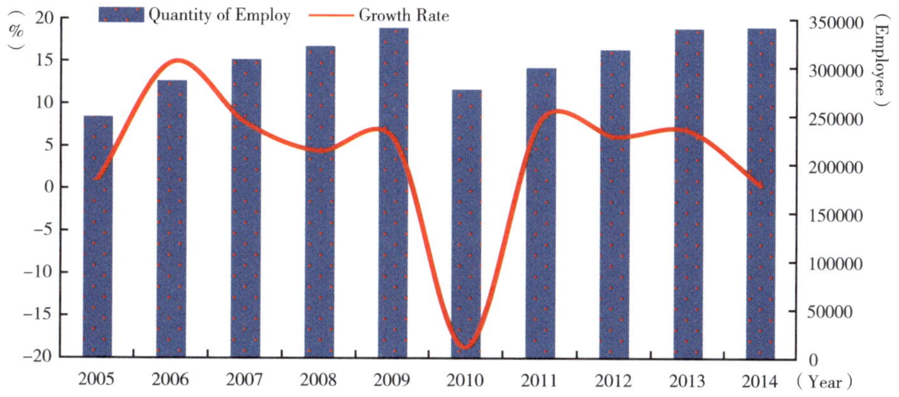

Graph 2-17 The number of employees in Chinese travel agencies in 2005-2014

college or higher degrees in travel agencies became larger and larger – it grew from 61.63% in 2010 to 71.31% in 2014, and the growth range was nearly 10%. Therefore, more and more people who are high educated and professionally trained would like to enter this industry. It can meet the need of industry transformation and upgrading, and the market.

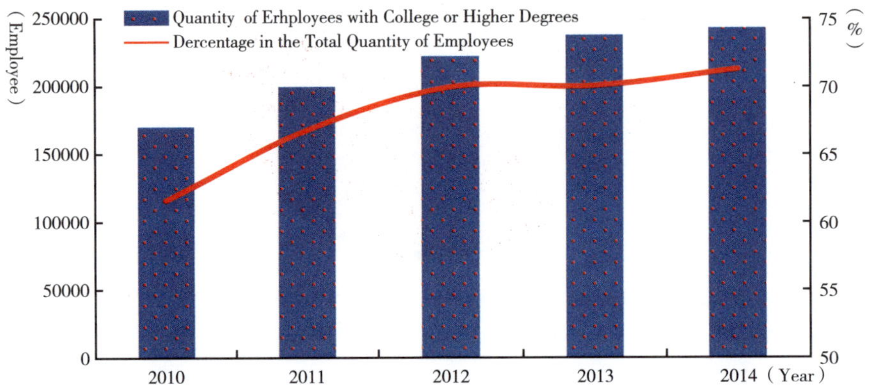

Graph 2–18 The number of employees with college or higher degrees in Chinese travel agencies in 2010–2014

Chapter III

Itemed Business Analysis on Chinese Travel Agency Industry

I. Domestic Tourism Business

In 2014, there were 131.1666 million trips those were organized to travel in China, with 415.4583 million people a day; and 144.5777 million trips were received, with 349.7844 million people a day. It respectively increased 2.03% and 1.72%, reduced 0.43% and increased 3.40% from the year earlier.

In 2014, the situation of domestic group tours reception was better than that of 2013, while the growth speed was still slow, and the number of received trips kept declining. Compared with domestic trips with a double-digit growth, the above data shows that more and more domestic tourists choose to travel alone instead of traveling with travel agencies.

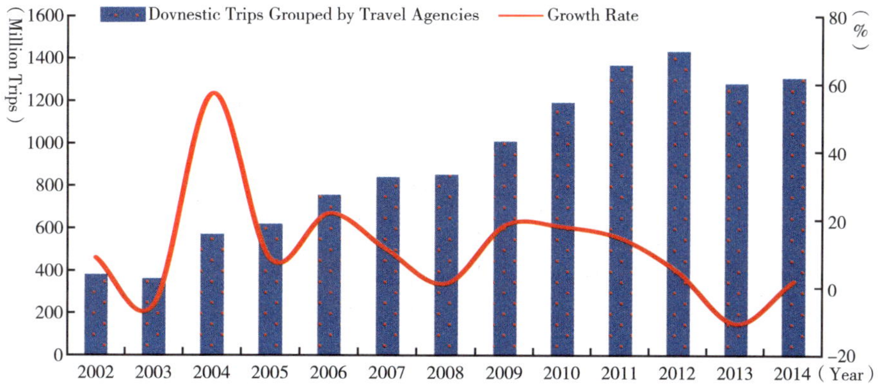

Graph 3-1 Domestic trips and growth rate of Chinese travel agencies in 2002-2014

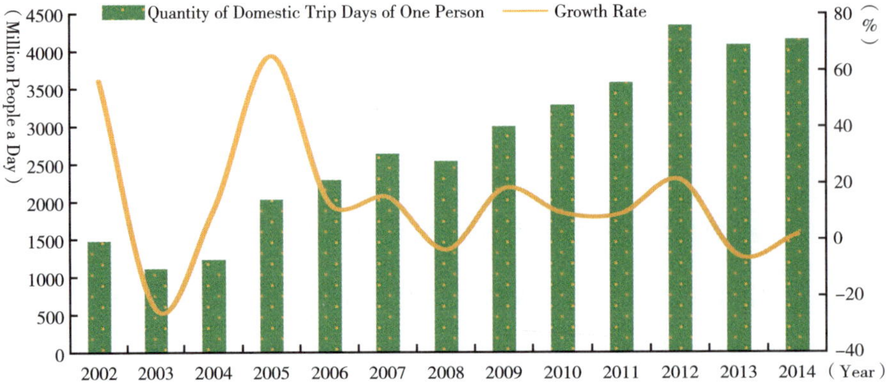

Graph 3–2 The number of domestic trip days of one person and growth rate of Chinese travel agencies in 2002–2014

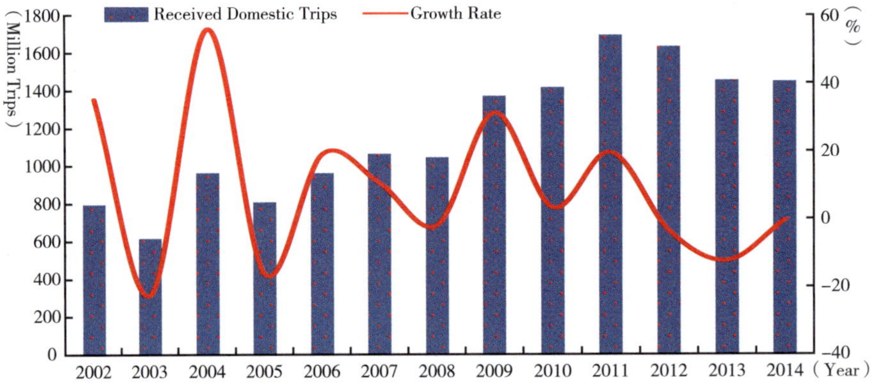

Graph 3–3 Received domestic trips and growth rate of Chinese travel agencies in 2002–2014

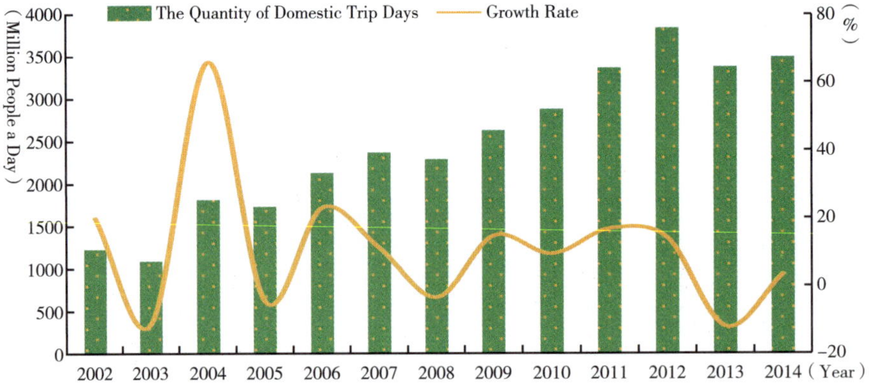

Graph 3–4 The number of domestic trip days and growth rate of Chinese travel agencies in 2002–2014

In 2014, the top 10 provinces (municipalities and autonomous regions) in the list of domestic organized trips of Chinese travel agencies were Guangdong, Jiangsu, Zhejiang, Shandong, Shanghai, Hubei, Chongqing, Fujian, Liaoning and Hunan in turn.

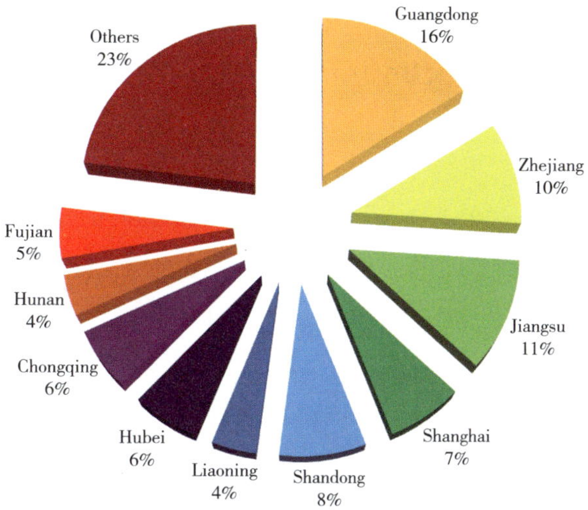

Graph 3-5 The top 10 provinces of domestic organized trips in 2014

In 2014, Beijing dropped out of the top 10 list and the city instead it was Liaoning. Although Guangzhou's share slightly dropped, it still ranked the first place. There was no change in the composition of the top three.

In 2014, the top 10 provinces (municipalities and autonomous regions) in the list of domestic received trips of Chinese travel agencies were Jiangsu, Zhejiang, Guangdong, Fujian, Hubei, Shandong, Yunnan, Chongqing, Shanghai and Sichuan in turn.

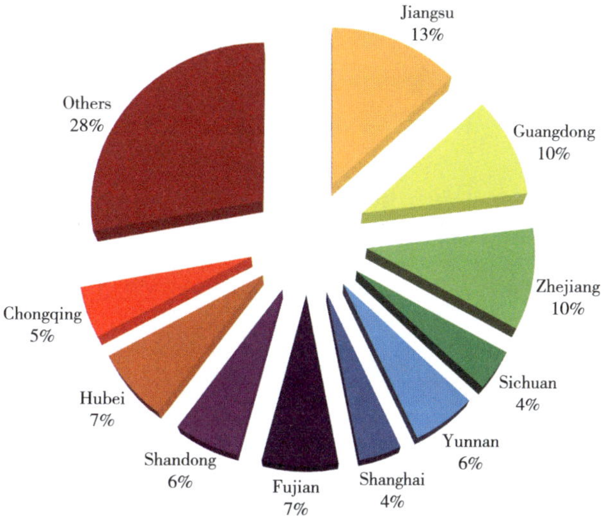

Graph 3-6 The top 10 provinces of domestic received trips in 2014

In 2014, Sichuan entered the top 10 list instead of Hunan; Yunnan glided two places, and Jiangsu still ranked the first place. There also was no change in the composition of the top three.

II. Outbound Tourism Business

In 2014, there were 39.1498 million trips those were organized to travel abroad, with 209.1177 million people a day; they respectively increased 16.67% and 24.74% from the year earlier. In this year, under the good conditions of domestic economic and social development, coupled with RMB appreciation and the convenient policy published by every region, Chinese outbound tourism continued to grow rapidly, but the growth rate was in a state of falling back.

Graph 3–7　Outbound trips and growth rate of Chinese travel agencies in 2002–2014

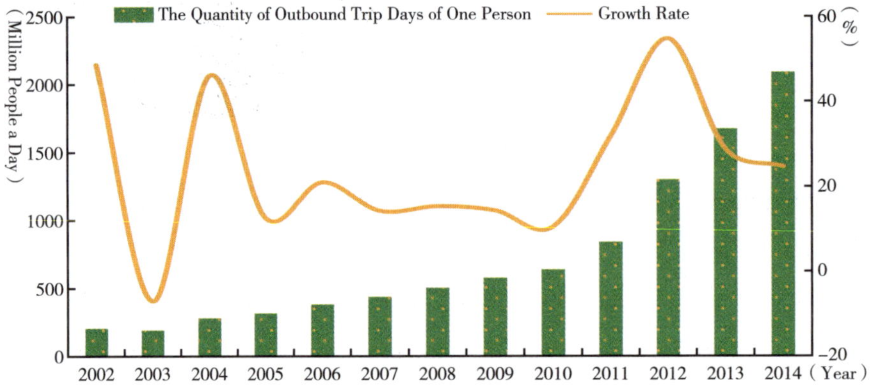

Graph 3–8　The number of outbound trip days of one person and growth rate of Chinese travel agencies in 2002–2014

In 2014, the top 10 countries and regions in the list of outbound received trips of Chinese travel agencies were Hong Kong, South Korea, Thailand, Taiwan, Macao, Japan, Singapore, Malaysia, Indonesia and France in turn.

In recent years, some countries such as Japan and South Korea are simplifying their visa procedures and shopping preferential policies to attract Chinese tourists. In 2014, South Korea surpassed Thailand, and became the second place in the list of outbound received trips - Japan promoted two places, became sixth; Hong Kong still ranked first, but its share declined; Indonesia replaced Vietnam to enter the list.

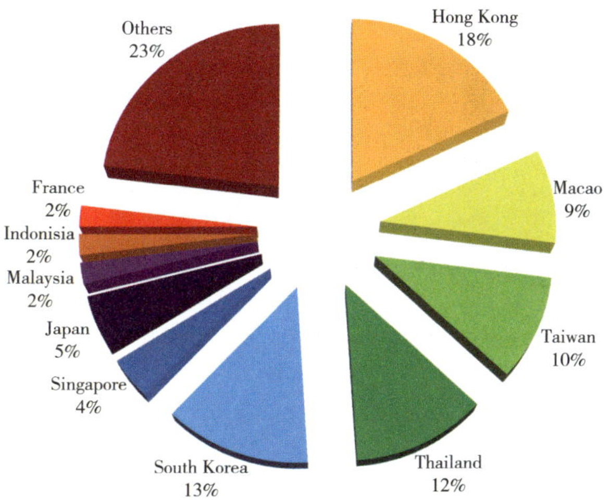

Graph 3–9 The top 10 destination countries and regions of outbound organized trips in 2014

III. Inbound Tourism Business

In 2014, there were 14.1004 million trips those were organized to travel abroad, with 61.6594 million people a day; and 20.0256 million trips were received, with 68.5515 million people a day. It respectively reduced 2.59%, increased1.69%, reduced 2.18% and increased 2.81% from the year earlier.

In 2014, due to that the global economy had not yet fully recovered, Chinese tour price were less competitive, and all countries and regions strengthened the efforts to scramble for tourist sources. The development of Chinese inbound tourism enters the mature stage, and cannot adapt to the new pattern of current international tourism, combined with the bad influence of the fog and environmental pollution, inbound tourism market is still in fatigue.

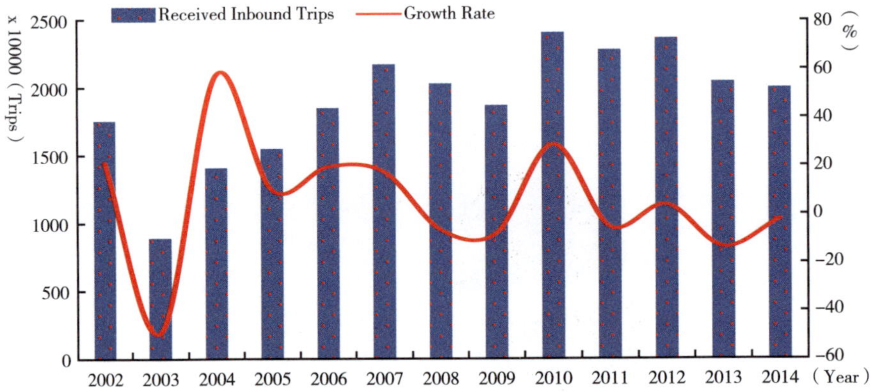

Graph 3-10 Received inbound trips and growth rate of Chinese travel agencies in 2002-2014

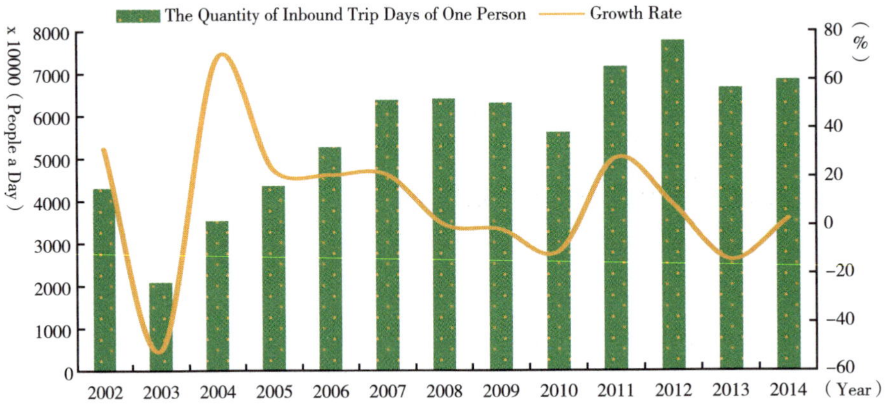

Graph 3-11 The number of inbound trip days of one person and growth rate of Chinese travel agencies in 2002-2014

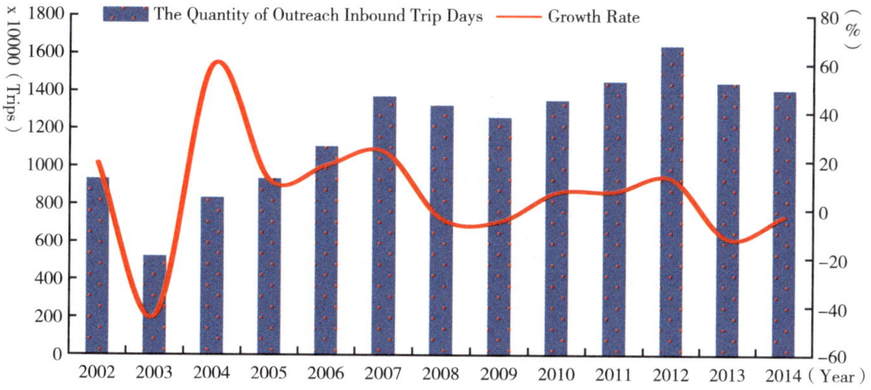

Graph 3–12 The number of outreach inbound trip days and growth rate of Chinese travel agencies in 2002–2014

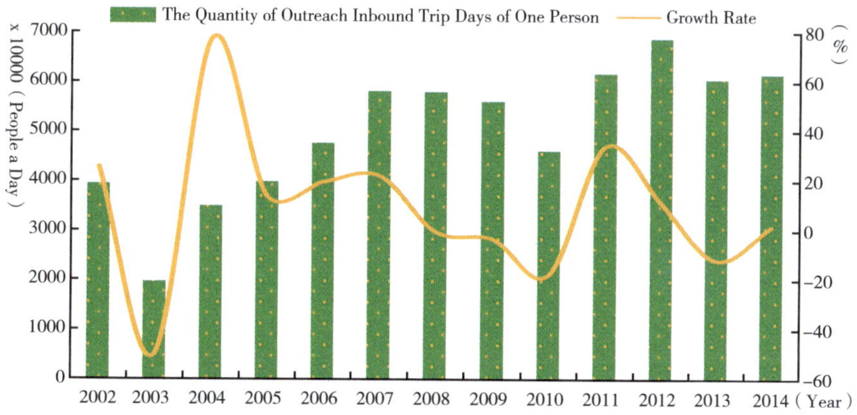

Graph 3–13 The number of outreach inbound trip days of one person and growth rate of Chinese travel agencies in 2002–2014

In 2014, the top 10 countries and regions in the list of outreach inbound trips of travel agencies were Hong Kong, Taiwan, South Korea, Macao, Singapore, United State, Russia, Japan, Malaysia and Thailand in turn.

In 2014, the passenger source pattern (countries or regions) of outreach inbound tourism of Chinese travel agencies was relatively stable. Hong Kong was in the first place, and Taiwan and South Korea placed respectively second and third. Macao's share slightly increased, still in the fourth. Singapore raised a place, in the fifth.

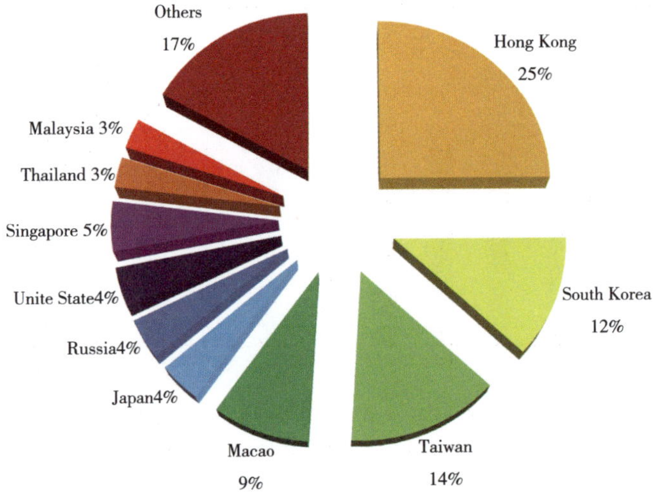

Graph 3–14 The top 10 tourist resource countries and regions of outreach inbound trips in 2014

In 2014, the top 10 tourist resource countries and regions of received inbound trips were Hong Kong, Taiwan, South Korea, Macao, United State, Russia, Singapore, Malaysia, Thailand and Japan in turn.

In 2014, the top 6 tourist resource countries and regions of received inbound trips

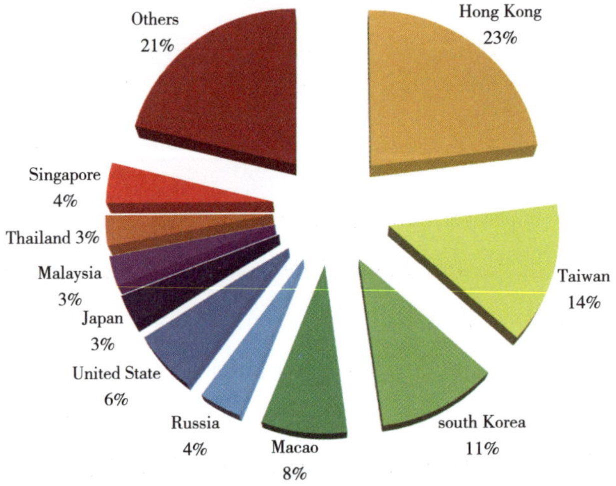

Graph 3–15 The top 10 tourist resource countries and regions of inbound trips in 2014

did not change. The share of Hong Kong, Macao and Taiwan increased; that of Thailand fell by 2%, with two places declined; Singapore rose two places; and Japan was still in the bottom.

IV. Comparison of Itemized Business

4.1 Comparison of trips in three main markets in 2014

Compared three indicators data of inbound outreach trips, domestic organized trips and outbound organized trips, the share percentage of inbound tourism, domestic tourism and outbound tourism in 2014 were respectively 8%, 71% and 21%, and kept the same, reduced 2% and increased 2% respectively from the year earlier.

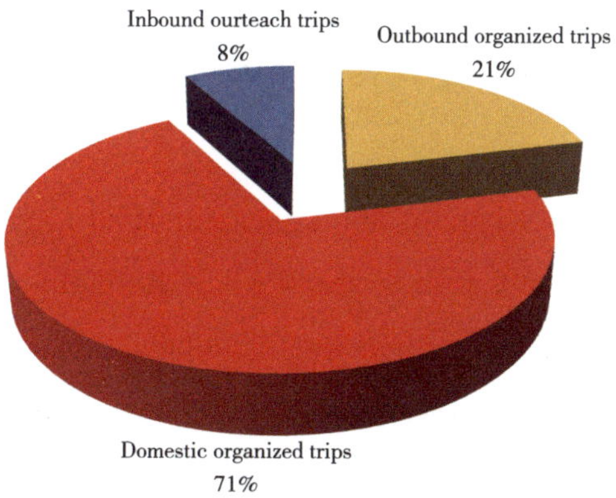

Graph 3-16 Comparison of trips in three main markets in 2014

4.2 Comparison of the number of days for each person in three main markets in 2014

Compared three indicators data of inbound outreach days of one person, domestic organized days of one person and outbound organized days of one person, the share percentage of inbound tourism, domestic tourism and outbound tourism in 2014 were respectively 9%, 61% and 30%, and reduced 1%, reduced 3% and increased 4% respectively from the year earlier.

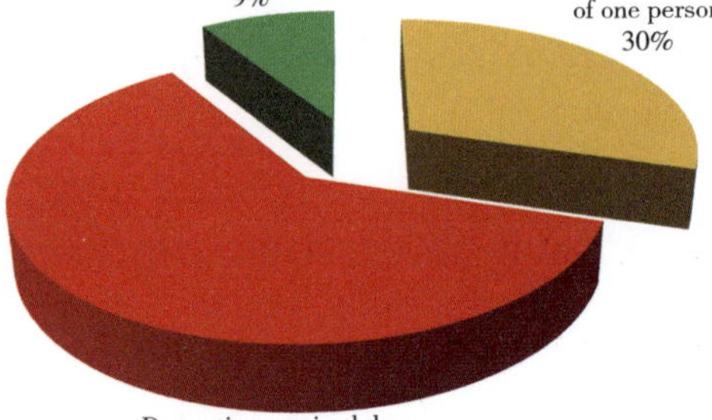

Graph 3–17 Comparison of the number of days for each person in three main markets in 2014

4.3 Comparison of business revenues in three main markets in 2014

In 2014, the business revenue of domestic tourism of Chinese travel agencies was 185.069 billion yuan, up 5.03% from a year earlier, accounting for 53.05% of the total business revenue of Chinese travel agencies. The domestic tourism business profit was 9.191 billion yuan, up 4.42% from a year earlier, accounting for 53.35% of the total business profit.

In 2014, the business revenue of outbound tourism was 135.466 billion yuan, up 17.07% from a year earlier, accounting for 38.83% of the total business revenue of Chinese travel agencies. The outbound tourism business profit was 6.436 billion yuan, up 8.23% from a year earlier, accounting for 37.36% of the total business profit.

In 2014, the business revenue of inbound tourism was 28.304 billion yuan, up 4.77% from a year earlier, accounting for 8.11% of the total business revenue of Chinese travel agencies. The inbound tourism business profit was 1.601 billion yuan, up 8.17% from a year earlier, accounting for 9.29% of the total business profit.

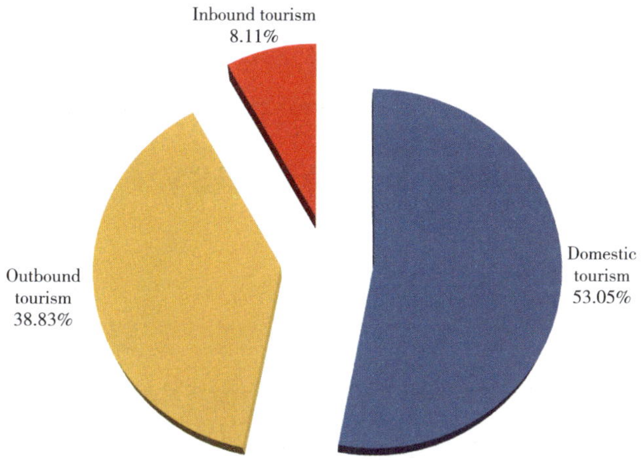

Graph 3-18 The percentage of business revenues in three main tourism markets in 2014

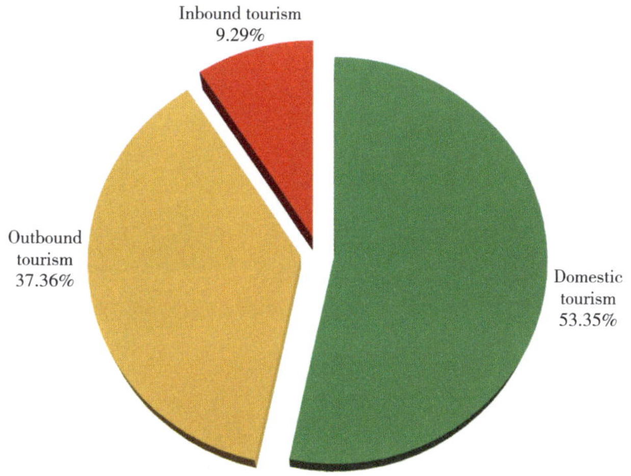

Graph 3-19 The percentage of business profits in three main tourism markets in 2014

Chapter IV

Analysis on Regional Market of Chinese Travel Agency Industry

I. Industry Analysis on East China (Beijing, Tianjin, Hebei, Shanxi and Inner Mongolia)

1.1 Quantity of travel agencies

In 2014, there were 4680 travel agencies in east China, accounting for 17.56% of the total number of Chinese travel agencies. In the distribution, the quantity of travel agencies

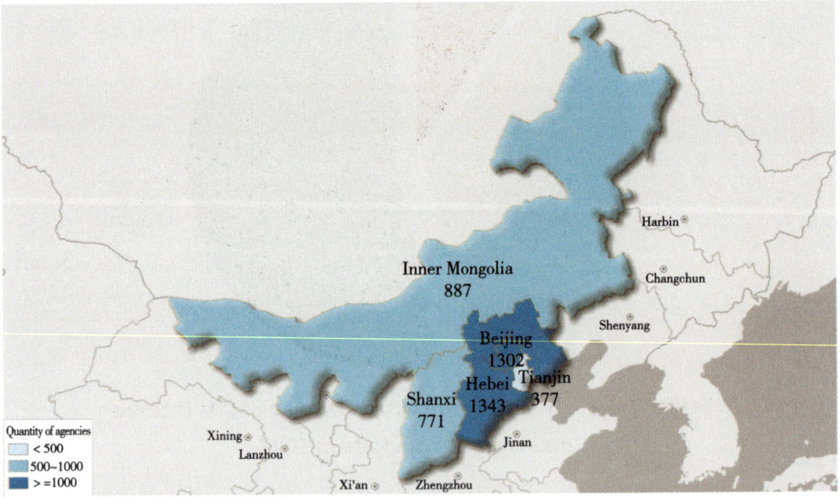

Graph 4–1 Distribution of the quantity of travel agencies in east China in 2014

地图来源：国家测绘局网站，审图号：GS（2014）6070 号

in east China was quite different in each part. Among them, there were more than 1000 travel agencies in Beijing and Hebei province, accounting for 56.52% together. There were respectively 887 and 771 travel agencies in Inner Mongolia and Shanxi, accounting for 18.95% and 16.47% respectively. It is notable that Tianjin had the most little quantity of travel agencies – only 377, accounting for 8.06%.

1.2 Tourism business revenue

In 2014, the tourism business revenue of travel agencies in north China was 61.381 billion yuan, accounting for 18.06% of the total tourism business revenue. In the tourism business revenue of each region in north China, Beijing was the best, whose tourism business revenue was 48.13 billion yuan, accounting for more than 78.41%. The tourism business revenues in Shanxi, Hebei and Tianjin achieved 4.883 billion yuan, 4.137 billion yuan and 2.498 billion yuan in a whole year, totally accounting for 18.76%. Inner Mongolia had the lowest revenue, only 1.733 billion yuan, accounting for more than 2.82%.

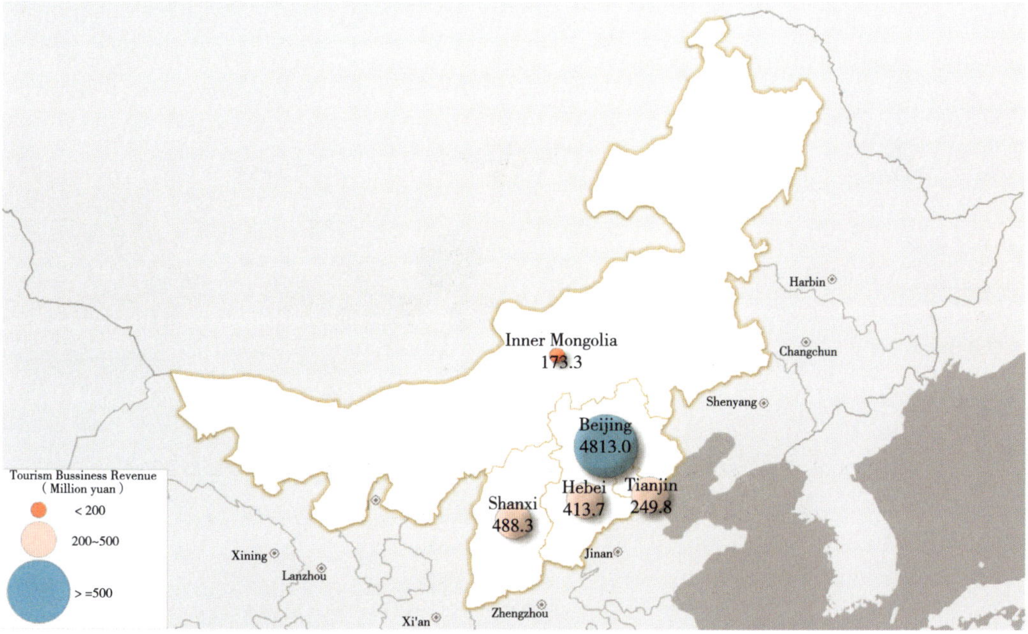

Graph 4–2 Distribution of the quantity of travel agencies in north China in 2014

地图来源：国家测绘局网站，审图号：GS（2014）6070 号

1.3 Tourism business profits

In 2014, the tourism business profit of travel agencies in north China was 2.998 billion yuan, accounting for 17.60% of the total Chinese tourism business profit. In the distribution of tourism business profit in north China, Beijing was still highlighted, who achieved the tourism business profit of 2.3 billion yuan, accounting for more than 76.72%. Hebei in the second place, its tourist business profit was 276 million yuan, accounting for more than 9.21%. All of profits in Tianjin, Shanxi and Inner Mongolia had not reached 200 million yuan, and those were 125 million yuan, 147 million yuan and 150 million yuan respectively, totally accounting for more than 14.07%.

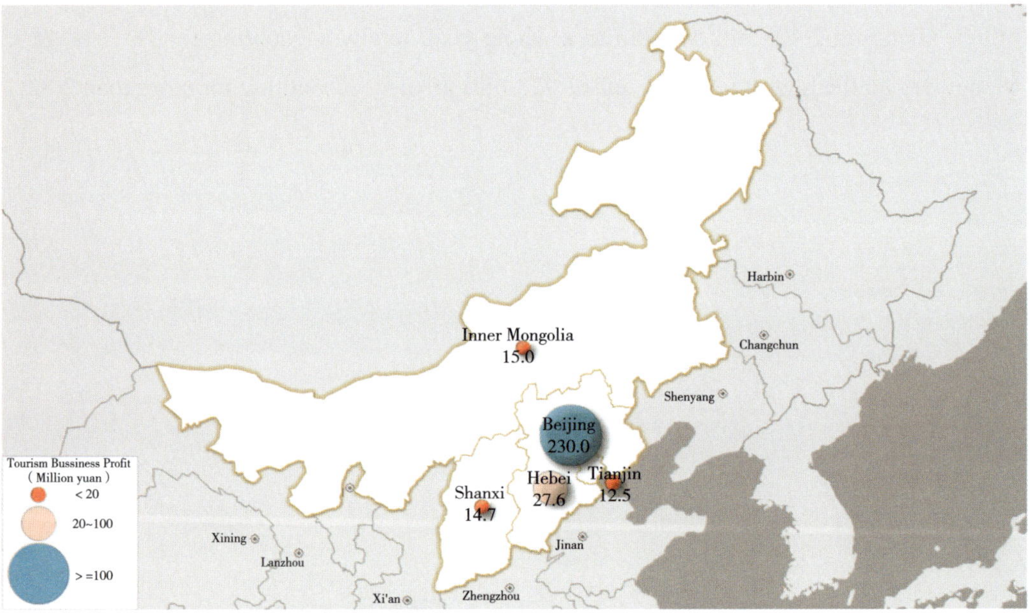

Graph 4-3 Distribution of tourism business profit in north China in 2014

地图来源：国家测绘局网站，审图号：GS（2014）6070 号

II. Industry Analysis on Northeast China (Heilongjiang , Jilin and Liaoning)

2.1 Quantity of travel agencies

In 2014, there were 2455 travel agencies in northeast China, accounting for 9.21% of the total number of Chinese travel agencies. In the distribution of the quantity of travel agencies in northeast China, Liaoning occupied half of them, which had 1210 travel agencies, accounting for 49.29%. Heilongjiang with 663 travel agencies, was the second, accounting for 27%. Jilin had the least travel agencies with the quantity of 582, accounting for 23.71%.

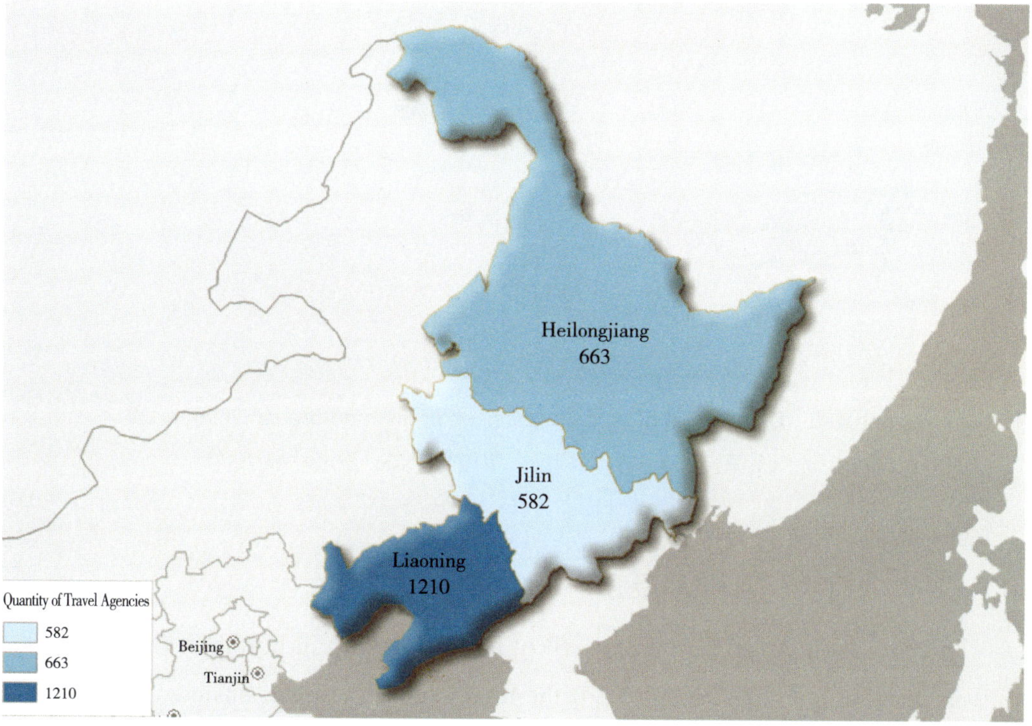

Graph 4-4 Distribution of the quantity of travel agencies in northeast China in 2014

地图来源：国家测绘局网站，审图号：GS（2014）6070 号

2.2 Tourism business revenue

In 2014, the tourism business revenue of travel agencies in northeast China was 16.218 billion yuan, accounting for 4.77% of the total tourism business revenue. In the percentage of tourism business revenue of each region in northeast China, Liaoning was the best, whose tourism business revenue was 11.125 billion yuan, accounting for 68.60%, close to 70%. The second was Heilongjiang, whose tourism business revenue was 3.707 billion yuan, accounting for 22.85%. And Jilin had the least revenue of 1.386 billion yuan, accounting for 8.55%.

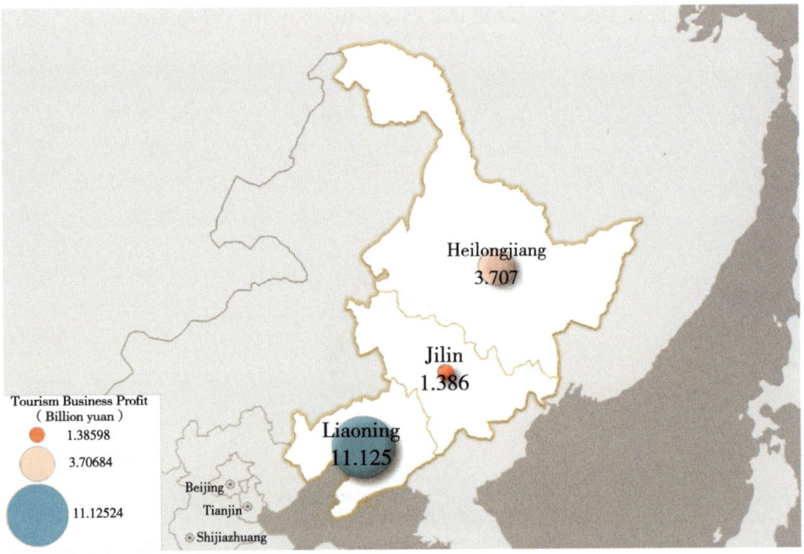

Graph 4-5 Distribution of tourism business profit in northeast China in 2014

地图来源：国家测绘局网站，审图号：GS（2014）6070 号

2.3 Tourism business profits

In 2014, the tourism business profit of travel agencies in northeast China was 854 million yuan, accounting for 5.01% of the total Chinese tourism business profit. In the distribution of tourism business profits in northeast China, Liaoning still achieved the highest with the tourism business profit of 605 million yuan, accounting for 70.84%. The second was Heilongjiang, whose tourist business profit was 224 million yuan, accounting for 26.23%. Jilin only had the profit of 25 million yuan, accounting for less than 3%.

Graph 4–6 Distribution of tourism business profit in northeast China in 2014

地图来源：国家测绘局网站，审图号：GS（2014）6070 号

III. Industry Analysis on East China (Shandong, Jiangsu, Anhui, Zhejiang, Fujian, Jiangxi and Shanghai)

3.1 Quantity of travel agencies

In 2014, there were 9976 travel agencies in east China, accounting for 37.43% of the total number of Chinese travel agencies. In the distribution of the quantity of travel agencies in east China, Shandong, Jiangsu and Zhejiang had more than 2000 agencies, and their quantities were 20542099 and 2036 respectively, totally accounting for 62.04%. Shanghai and Anhui had more than 1000 agencies, and their quantities were 1185 and 1046 respectively, totally accounting for 22.36%. Fujian and Jiangxi had less than 1000 agencies, and their quantities were 805 and 751 respectively, totally accounting for 15.60%.

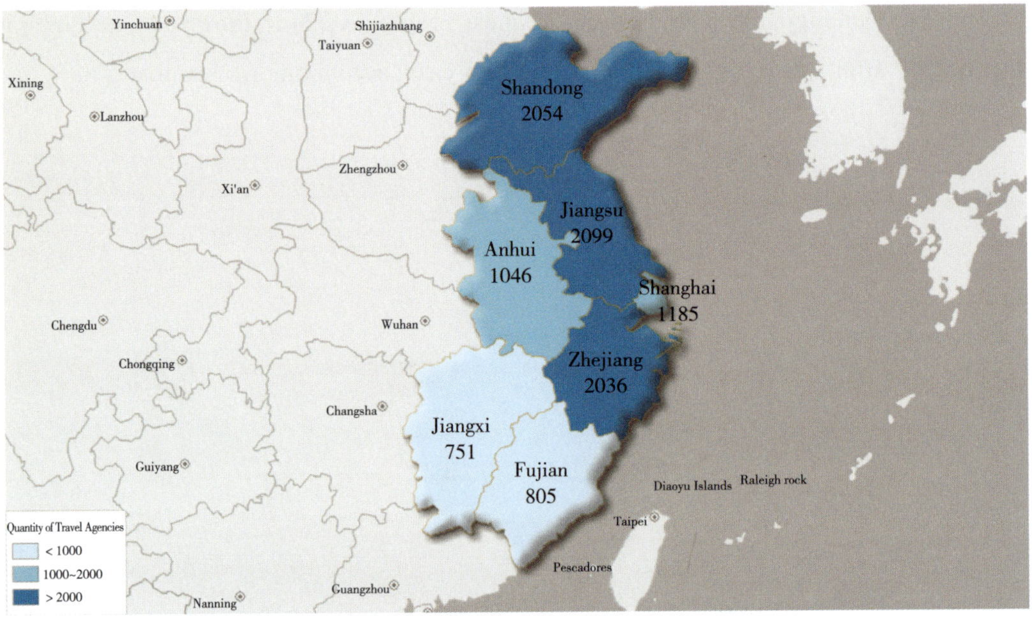

Graph 4-7 Distribution of the quantity of travel agencies in east China in 2014

地图来源：国家测绘局网站，审图号：GS（2014）6070 号

3.2 Tourism business revenue

In 2014, the tourism business revenue of travel agencies in east China was 135.390 billion yuan, accounting for 39.84% of the total tourism business revenue. In the distribution of regions in east China, it could be divided into four levels. The first one was Shanghai who had tourism business revenue of 51.022 billion yuan, accounting for 37.69%; the second one included Jiangsu and Zhejiang, their revenues were respectively 22.738 and 22.417 billion yuan - all more than 20 billion yuan - totally accounting for 33.35%; the third one included Shandong and Fujian, their revenues were respectively 15.659 and 15.099 billion yuan - all more than 15 billion yuan - totally accounting for 22.72%; and the forth one included Anhui and Jiangxi, their revenues were respectively 5.237 and 3.219 billion yuan, totally accounting for 6.25%.

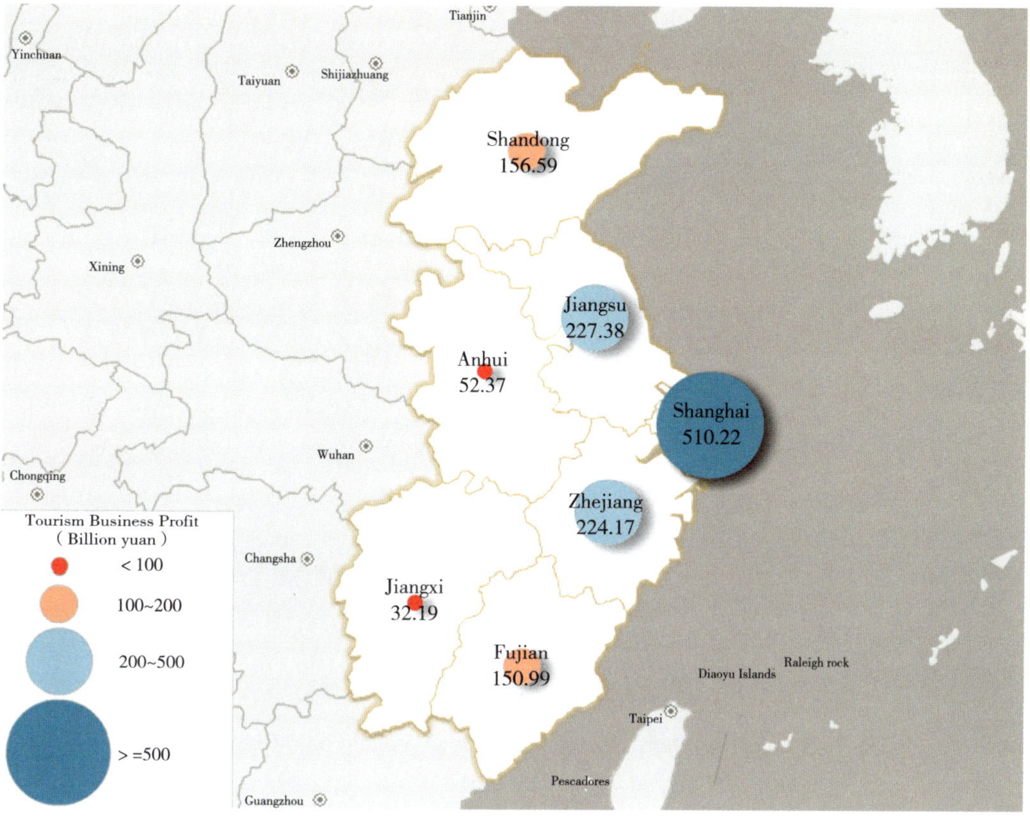

Graph 4–8 Distribution of tourism business profit in east China in 2014

地图来源：国家测绘局网站，审图号：GS（2014）6070 号

3.3 Tourism business profits

In 2014, the tourism business profit of travel agencies in east China was 6.405 billion yuan, accounting for 37.60% of the total Chinese tourism business profit. Shanghai was the best, who achieved 1.919 billion yuan, accounting for 29.96%. All of the profits of Zhejiang, Shandong and Jiangsu were more than 1 billion yuan, there were 1.114, 1.056 and 1.041 billion yuan respectively, accounting for 17.39%, 16.49% and 16.25%. And those of Fujian, Anhui and Shanxi were less than 1 billion yuan – 770348 and 157 million yuan respectively, totally accounting for 19.91%.

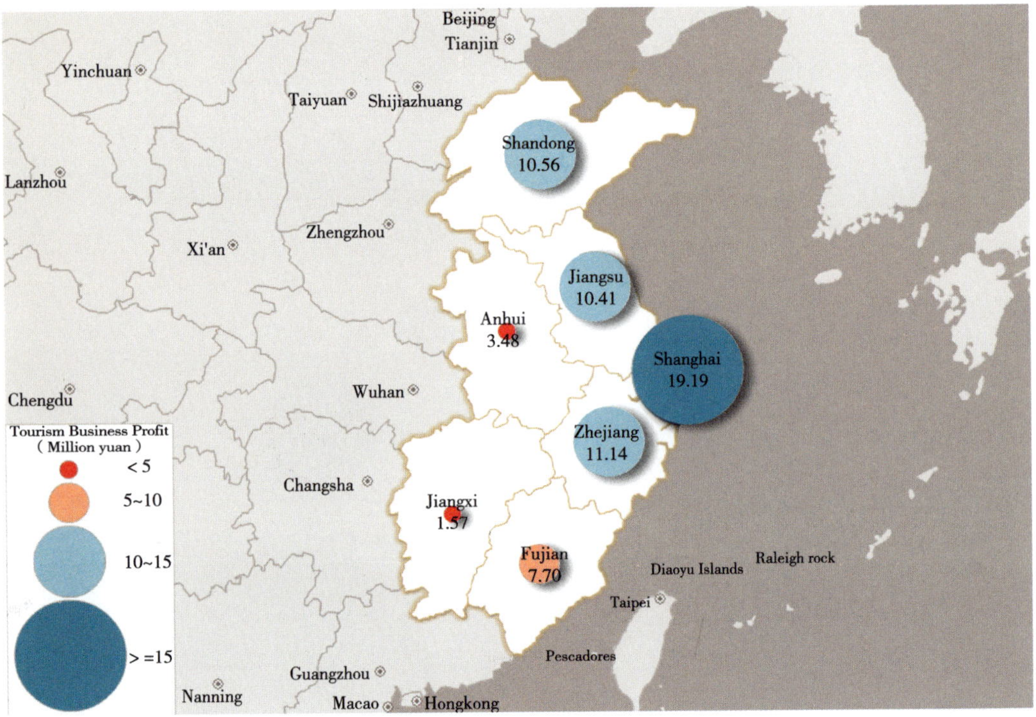

Graph 4–9 Distribution of tourism business profit in east China in 2014

地图来源：国家测绘局网站，审图号：GS（2014）6070 号

IV. Industry Analysis on South China (Guangdong, Guangxi and Hainan)

4.1 Quantity of travel agencies

In 2014, there were 2681 travel agencies in south China, accounting for 10.06% of the total number of Chinese travel agencies. In the distribution of the quantity, Guangdong had the largest quantity with 1792 agencies, accounting for 66.84%. Guangxi was in the second place, which had 537 agencies, accounting for 20.03%. And Hainan was the last with a quantity of 352 agencies, accounting for 13.13%.

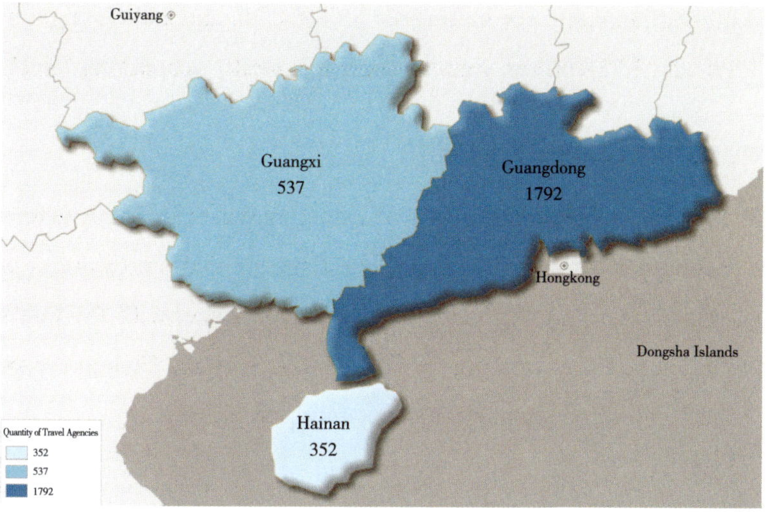

Graph 4–10 Distribution of the quantity of travel agencies in south China in 2014

地图来源：国家测绘局网站，审图号：GS（2014）6070 号

4.2 Tourism business revenue

In 2014, the tourism business revenue of travel agencies in south China was 60.891 billion yuan, accounting for 17.92% of the total tourism business revenue. In the distribution of regions, Guangdong had a highlight performance with the tourism business

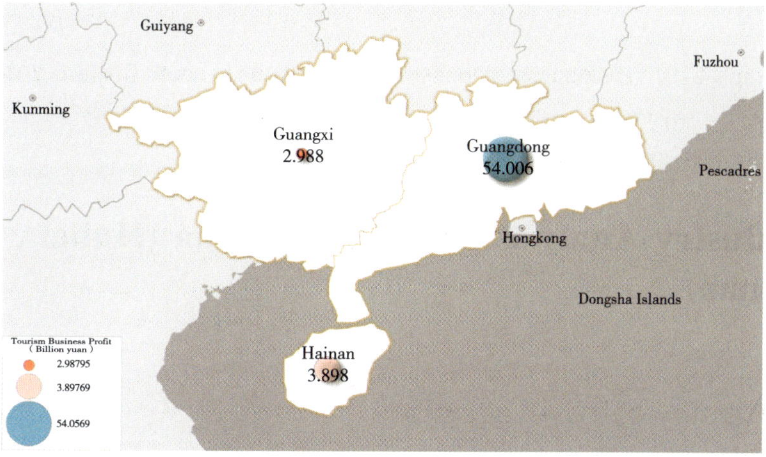

Graph 4–11 Distribution of tourism business profit in south China in 2014

地图来源：国家测绘局网站，审图号：GS（2014）6070 号

revenue of 54.006 billion yuan, accounting for 88.69%. Hainan and Guangxi had achieved revenues of 3.898 and 2.988 billion yuan respectively, totally accounting for 11.31%.

4.3 Tourism business profits

In 2014, the tourism business profit of travel agencies in south China was 3.602 billion yuan, accounting for 21.15% of the total Chinese tourism business profit. In the distribution of regions, Guangdong made a good performance, with the tourism business profit of 3.266 billion yuan, accounting for 90.67 %. Hainan and Guangxi respectively had profits of 182 and 155 million yuan, totally accounting for 9.33%.

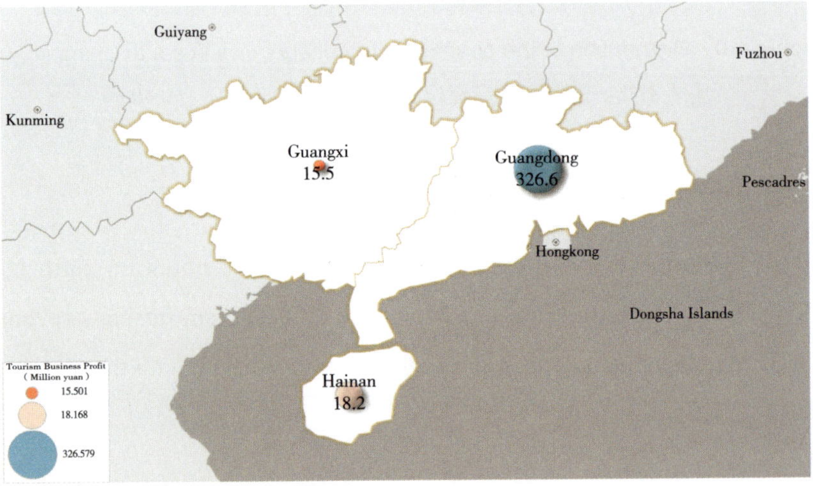

Graph 4–12 Distribution of tourism business profit in south China in 2014

地图来源：国家测绘局网站，审图号：GS（2014）6070 号

V. Industry Analysis on Central China (Hubei , Hunan, Henan)

5.1 Quantity of travel agencies

In 2014, there were 2901 travel agencies in central China, accounting for 10.89% of the total number of Chinese travel agencies. In the distribution of the quantity, both Henan and Hubei had more than 1000 agencies – 1100 and 1050 agencies respectively, accounting for 37.92% and 36.19%. Hunan had the quantity of 751 agencies, accounting for 25.89%.

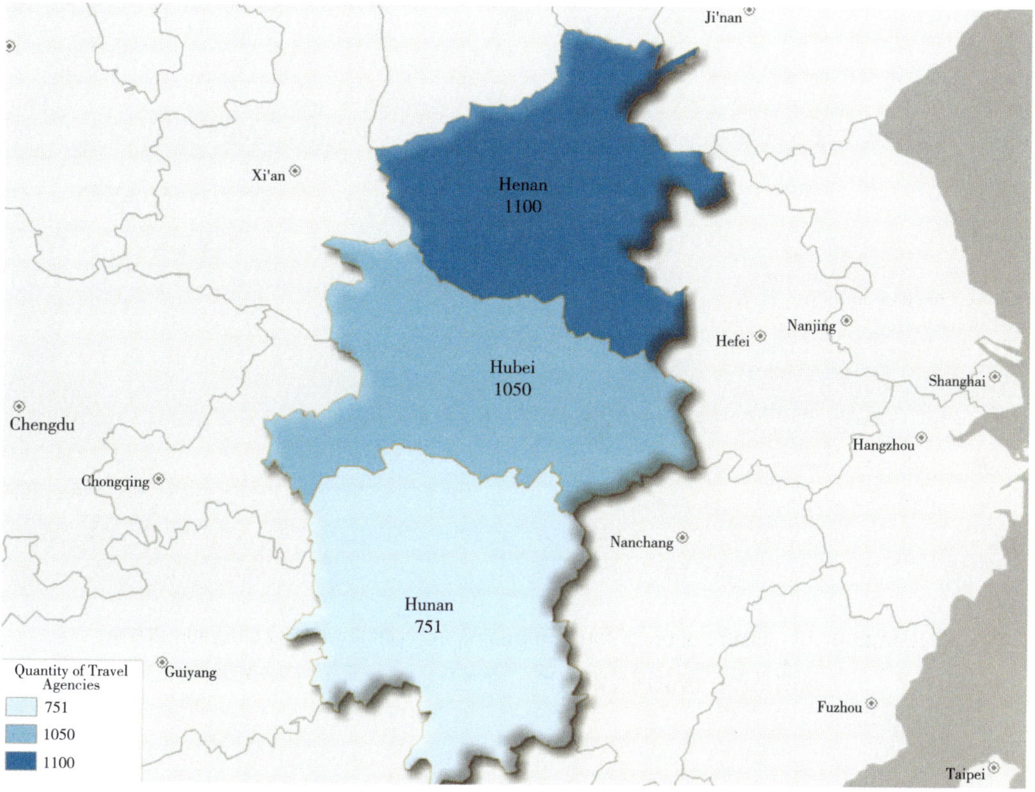

Graph 4-13 Distribution of the quantity of travel agencies in central China in 2014

地图来源：国家测绘局网站，审图号：GS（2014）6070 号

5.2 Tourism business revenue

In 2014, the tourism business revenue of travel agencies in central China was 27.125 billion yuan, accounting for 7.98% of the total tourism business revenue. In the distribution of regions, Hubei and Hunan had tourism business revenues of 11.824 and 11.396 billion yuan respectively, and they accounted for 43.59% and 42.01%. Henan only had revenue of 3.905 billion yuan, accounting for 14.40%.

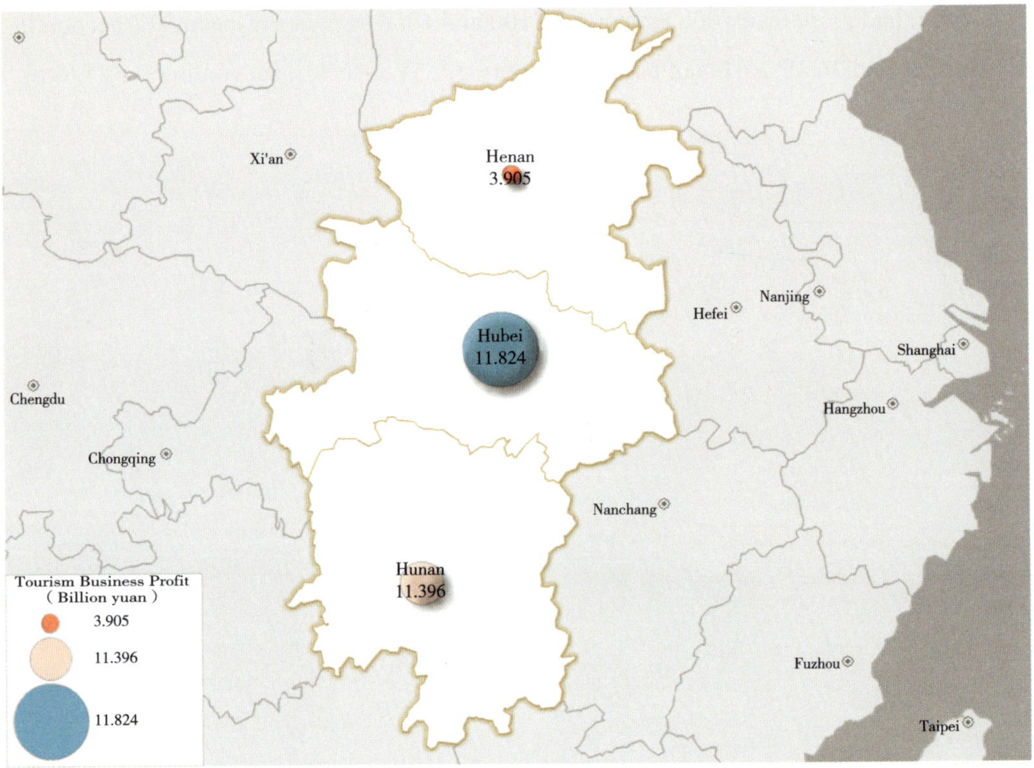

Graph 4-14 Distribution of tourism business profit in central China in 2014

地图来源：国家测绘局网站，审图号：GS（2014）6070 号

5.3 Tourism business profits

In 2014, the tourism business profit of travel agencies in central China was 1.399 billion yuan, accounting for 8.21% of the total Chinese tourism business profit. In the distribution of regions, Hubei had the tourism business profit of 661 million yuan while Hunan achieved 569 million yuan, respectively accounting for 47.25% and 40.67%. Henan had achieved the profit of 169 million yuan, accounting for only 12.08%.

Graph 4–15 Distribution of tourism business profit in central China in 2014

地图来源：国家测绘局网站，审图号：GS（2014）6070 号

VI. Industry Analysis on Southwest China (Sichuan, Yunnan, Guizhou, Tibet and Chongqing)

6.1 Quantity of travel agencies

In 2014, there were 2066 travel agencies in southwest China, accounting for 7.75% of the total number of Chinese travel agencies. In the distribution of the quantity, Yunnan had 704 agencies and Chongqing had 504, respectively accounting for 34.08% and 24.39%. Sichuan, Guizhou and Tibet had 457, 299 and 102 agencies respectively, totally accounting for 41.53%.

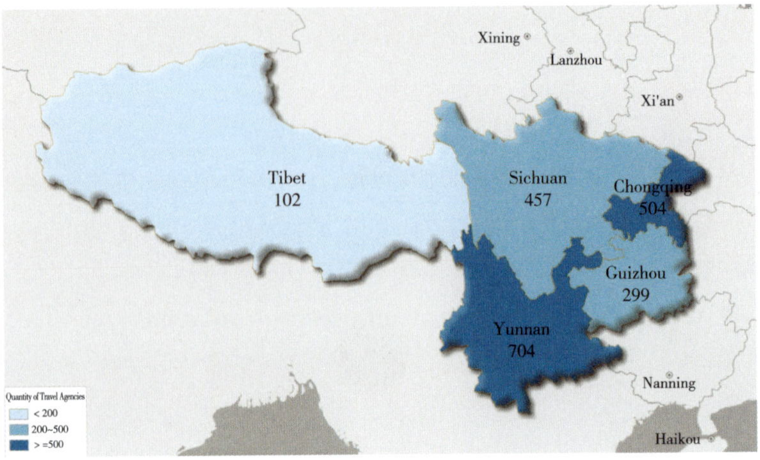

Graph 4–16 Distribution of the quantity of travel agencies in southwest China in 2014

地图来源：国家测绘局网站，审图号：GS（2014）6070 号

6.2 Tourism business revenue

In 2014, the tourism business revenue of travel agencies in southwest China was 28.138 billion yuan, accounting for 8.28% of the total tourism business revenue. Only Chongqing in southwest China in 2014 had the revenue of more than 10 billion yuan – 12.278 billion yuan, accounting for 43.63%. Yunnan and Sichuan had respectively 8.999 and 5.448 billion yuan, accounting for 31.98% and 19.36%. Guizhou and Tibet only had the revenues of 1.225

Graph 4–17 Distribution of tourism business profit in southwest China in 2014

地图来源：国家测绘局网站，审图号：GS（2014）6070 号

billion yuan and 187 million yuan, respectively accounting for 4.35% and 0.66%.

6.3 Tourism business profits

In 2014, the tourism business profit of travel agencies in southwest China was 1.191 billion yuan, accounting for 7.00% of the total Chinese tourism business profit. In the distribution of regions, only Chongqing had achieved the profit of more than 500 million yuan – 538 million yuan, accounting for 45.17%. The second one was Yunnan, with the profit of 482 million yuan, accounting for 40.47%. The profit of Sichuan and Guizhou were respectively 131 and 46 million yuan, totally accounting for 14.86%. However, Tibet was in red in 2014, with the loss of 5346600 yuan.

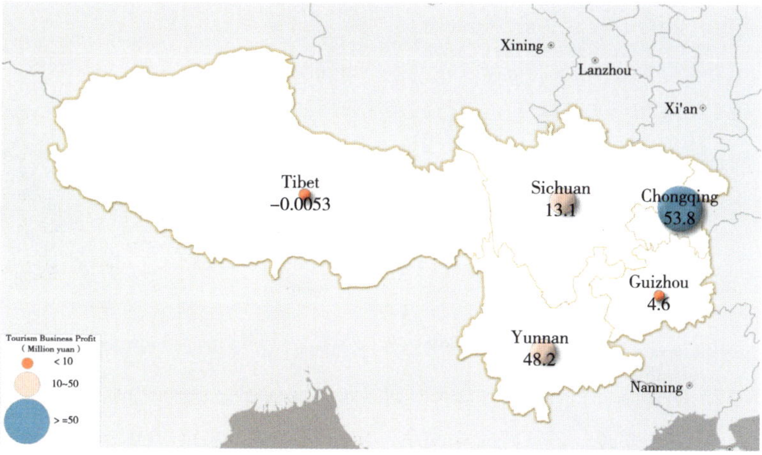

Graph 4–18 Distribution of tourism business profit in southwest China in 2014

地图来源：国家测绘局网站，审图号：GS（2014）6070 号

VII. Industry Analysis on Northwest China (Ningxia, Xinjiang, Qinghai, Shaanxi and Gansu)

7.1 Quantity of travel agencies

In 2014, there were 1891 travel agencies in southwest China (including Xinjiang Production and Construction Corps), accounting for 7.10% of the total number of

Chinese travel agencies. In this year, the only province who had more than 500 agencies was Shaanxi, with 687 agencies, accounting for 36.33%. Gansu, Xinjiang and Qinghai had 423338 and 237 agencies respectively, totally accounting for 52.78%. And Ningxia and Xinjiang Production and Construction Corps had respectively 114 and 92 agencies respectively, totally accounting for 10.89%.

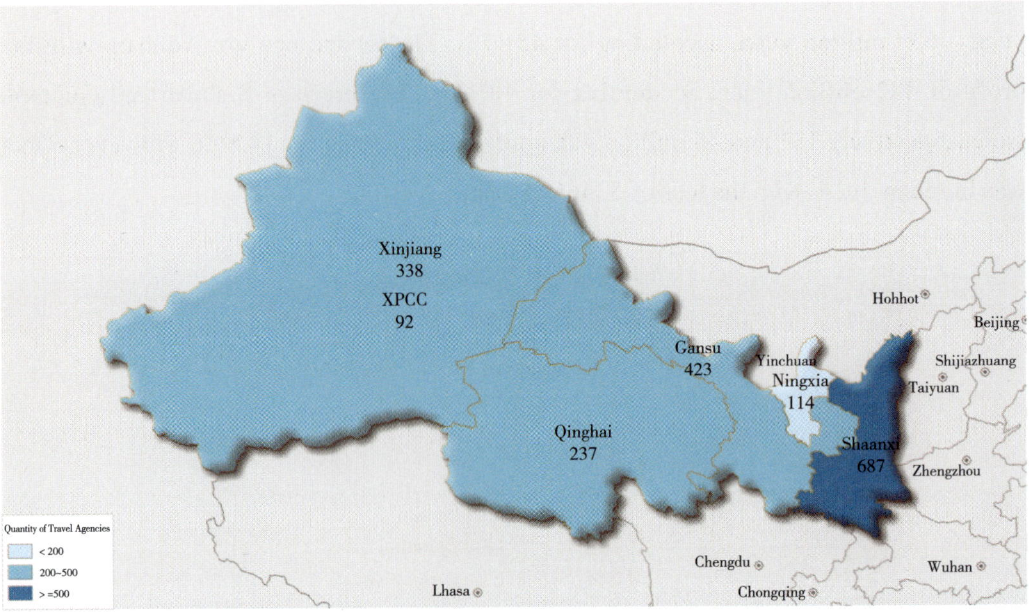

Graph 4–19 Distribution of the quantity of travel agencies in northwest China in 2014

地图来源：国家测绘局网站，审图号：GS（2014）6070 号

7.2 Tourism business revenue

In 2014, the tourism business revenue of travel agencies in northwest China (including Xinjiang Production and Construction Corps) was 10.661 billion yuan, accounting for 3.14% of the total tourism business revenue. In the distribution of regions, Shaanxi performed better than other provinces; its revenue was 5.85 billion yuan, accounting for 54.87%. The revenues of Gansu and Xinjiang were respectively 1.604 and 1.506 billion yuan, totally accounting for 29.17%. The tourism business revenues of Ningxia, Corps and Qinghai were respectively 60.7, 55.9 and 53.5 million yuan, totally accounting for 15.96%.

Graph 4–20 Distribution of tourism business profit in northwest China in 2014

地图来源：国家测绘局网站，审图号：GS（2014）6070 号

7.3 Tourism business profits

In 2014, the tourism business profit of travel agencies in northwest China (including Xinjiang Production and Construction Corps) was 582 million yuan, accounting for 3.42% of the total Chinese tourism business profit. In the distribution of regions, Shaanxi was still on the first place, with the profit of 394 million yuan, accounting for 67.70%. But the profit of Xinjiang, Qinghai, Gansu, Ningxia and Xinjiang Production and Construction Corps respectively were 46, 48, 39, 16 and 37 million yuan, totally accounting for 32.30%.

Graph 4–21 Distribution of tourism business profit in northwest China in 2014

地图来源：国家测绘局网站，审图号：GS（2014）6070 号

Part Ⅲ
附　录

2014 年度全国旅行社统计调查排强名单

依据《旅游法》《统计法》《旅行社条例》《旅行社条例实施细则》和《旅游统计调查制度》，国家旅游局组织开展了 2014 年度全国旅行社统计调查工作，依据 2014 年度全国旅行社统计调查指标和经营情况，按照 2014 年度全国旅行社统计调查排强标准，排出了 2014 年度全国百强旅行社、2014 年度全国入境二十强旅行社、2014 年度全国利税贡献二十强旅行社和 2014 年度全国旅行社集团二十强。

2014 年度全国百强旅行社

位次	许可证编号	旅行社名称
1	L-SH-CJ00009	上海春秋国际旅行社（集团）有限公司
2	L-BJ-CJ00003	中青旅控股股份有限公司
3	L-BJ-CJ00071	北京众信国际旅行社股份有限公司
4	L-BJ-CJ00051	北京凯撒国际旅行社有限责任公司
5	L-GD-CJ00004	广州广之旅国际旅行社股份有限公司
6	L-GD-CJ00002	广东省中国旅行社股份有限公司
7	L-BJ-CJ00043	竹园国际旅行社有限公司
8	L-CQ-CJ00001	重庆海外旅业（旅行社）集团有限公司
9	L-BJ-CJ00001	中国国际旅行社总社有限公司
10	L-HUB-CJ00019	湖北万达新航线国际旅行社有限责任公司
11	L-HUN-CJ00008	湖南海外旅游有限公司
12	L-ZJ-CJ00008	浙旅控股股份有限公司
13	L-BJ-CJ00020	北京凤凰假期国际旅行社有限公司

续表

位次	许可证编号	旅行社名称
14	L-GD-CJ00019	广东南湖国际旅行社有限责任公司
15	L-SH-CJ00057	中青旅（上海）国际会议展览有限公司
16	L-FJ-CJ00020	厦门建发国际旅行社有限公司
17	L-FJ-CJ00002	福建省中国旅行社
18	L-BJ-CJ00127	中青旅国际会议展览有限公司
19	L-SD-CJ00048	威海中国旅行社有限公司
20	L-SD-CJ00002	山东嘉华文化国际旅行社有限公司
21	L-HUB-CJ00022	中国国旅（宜昌）国际旅行社有限公司
22	L-SD-CJ00021	中国旅行社总社（青岛）有限公司
23	L-JS-CJ00001	中国国旅（江苏）国际旅行社有限公司
24	L-HUB-CJ00020	湖北康辉国际旅行社有限责任公司
25	L-CQ-CJ00002	重庆市中国旅行社（集团）有限公司
26	L-SD-CJ00016	港中旅国际（山东）旅行社有限公司
27	L-SD-CJ00046	山东南山国际旅行社有限公司
28	L-SX-CJ00041	山西宝华盛世国际旅行社有限公司
29	L-SH-CJ00005	上海锦江旅游有限公司
30	L-GD-CJ00052	深圳市海外国际旅行社有限公司
31	L-SH-CJ00004	上海中国青年旅行社
32	L-BJ-CJ00008	中国铁道旅行社
33	L-LN-CJ00002	沈阳市海外国际旅行社有限公司
34	L-HUN-CJ00002	湖南省万达亲和力旅游国际旅行社有限公司
35	L-BJ-CJ00011	中国康辉旅行社集团有限责任公司
36	L-HUB-CJ00035	湖北峡州国际旅行社有限公司
37	L-HEB-CJ00015	河北康辉国际旅行社有限责任公司
38	L-FJ-CJ00009	福建省春秋国际旅行社有限公司
39	L-FJ-CJ00042	中国国旅（福建）国际旅行社有限公司
40	L-SD-CJ00017	山东万达国际旅行社有限公司
41	L-AH-CJ00002	安徽中国青年旅行社有限责任公司
42	L-JX-CJ00006	南昌铁路国际旅行社有限责任公司

续表

位次	许可证编号	旅行社名称
43	L-LN-CJ00041	辽宁康辉国际旅行社有限公司
44	L-SD-CJ00010	山东交运旅游集团有限公司
45	L-FJ-CJ00008	福建省康辉国际旅行社股份有限公司
46	L-BJ-CJ00007	中国妇女旅行社
47	L-HUB-CJ00003	长江轮船海外旅游总公司
48	L-HUB-CJ00011	中南国际旅游公司（湖北）
49	L-LN-CJ00019	沈阳青年国际旅行社有限公司
50	L-BJ-CJ00114	北京迈途国际旅行社有限公司
51	L-SNX-CJ00004	陕西中国旅行社有限责任公司
52	L-ZJ-CJ00002	浙江省中国旅行社集团有限公司
53	L-SD-CJ00055	临沂国际旅行社有限公司
54	L-GD-CJ00082	广东顺之旅国际旅行社有限公司
55	L-LN-CJ00069	辽宁大运通国际旅行社有限公司
56	L-BJ-CJ00152	国旅国际会议展览有限公司
57	L-SX-CJ00034	山西红马国际旅行社有限公司
58	L-FJ-CJ00011	福建康泰国际旅行社有限公司
59	L-FJ-CJ00015	厦门旅游集团国际旅行社有限公司
60	L-ZJ-CJ00003	浙江省中青国际旅游有限公司
61	L-SD-CJ00098	东营市金桥国际旅行社有限责任公司
62	L-HUN-CJ00005	湖南新康辉国际旅行社有限责任公司
63	L-GD-CJ00115	中山中国国际旅行社有限公司
64	L-GD-CJ00081	佛山市禅之旅国际旅行社有限公司
65	L-GD-CJ00089	佛山市口岸国际旅行社有限公司
66	L-SNX-CJ00006	中国旅行社总社西北有限公司
67	L-AH-CJ00006	黄山市中国旅行社
68	L-SD-CJ00057	山东国际旅行社有限公司
69	L-SD-01018	山东省交通旅行社
70	L-FJ-CJ00005	福建省旅游有限公司
71	L-JX-CJ00007	江西光大国际旅行社有限公司

续表

位次	许可证编号	旅行社名称
72	L-HLJ-CJ00028	黑龙江天马国际旅行社有限公司
73	L-GD-CJ00001	中国国旅（广东）国际旅行社股份有限公司
74	L-SC-CJ00010	四川康辉国际旅行社有限公司
75	L-SH-CJ00045	中国旅行社总社（上海）有限公司
76	L-LN-CJ00020	辽宁世纪国际旅行社有限公司
77	L-SH-CJ00001	上海国旅国际旅行社有限公司
78	L-HEN-CJ00001	河南旅游集团有限公司
79	L-ZJ-CJ00063	浙江飞扬国际旅游集团有限公司
80	L-GD-CJ00056	深圳市宝中旅行社有限公司
81	L-AH-CJ00008	安徽万达环球国际旅行社有限责任公司
82	L-SD-CJ00022	青岛华青国际旅行社有限责任公司
83	L-BJ-CJ00202	北京海涛国际旅行社有限公司
84	L-BJ-CJ00288	北京沃凯德国际旅行有限公司
85	L-HLJ-CJ00017	哈尔滨俄风行国际旅行社有限公司
86	L-SD-CJ00001	山东旅游有限公司
87	L-GD-CJ00003	广东省中国青年旅行社
88	L-JS-CJ00012	江苏康辉国际旅行社有限责任公司
89	L-GD-CJ00041	深圳市口岸中国旅行社有限公司
90	L-JS-CJ00010	无锡市中国旅行社有限责任公司
91	L-LN-CJ00010	辽宁省中国青年旅行社有限公司
92	L-GD-CJ00044	深圳华侨城国际旅行社有限公司
93	L-CQ-CJ00020	重庆阳光国际旅行社有限公司
94	L-CQ-CJ00023	重庆新干线国际旅行社有限公司
95	L-FJ-CJ00034	福建省石狮市假日国际旅行社有限公司
96	L-JS-CJ00009	无锡中国国际旅行社有限公司
97	L-JS-CJ00018	中青旅江苏国际旅行社有限公司
98	L-BJ-CJ00005	中信旅游集团有限公司
99	L-GD-CJ00118	中山菊城假期国际旅行社有限公司
100	L-SC-CJ00002	成都中国青年旅行社

2014 年度全国入境二十强旅行社

位次	许可证编号	旅行社名称
1	L-BJ-CJ00001	中国国际旅行社总社有限公司
2	L-HUB-CJ00019	湖北万达新航线国际旅行社有限责任公司
3	L-FJ-CJ00005	福建省旅游有限公司
4	L-HUN-CJ00002	湖南省万达亲和力旅游国际旅行社有限公司
5	L-SD-CJ00022	青岛华青国际旅行社有限责任公司
6	L-SD-CJ00001	山东旅游有限公司
7	L-LN-CJ00002	沈阳市海外国际旅行社有限公司
8	L-BJ-CJ00086	中国旅行社总社（北京）有限公司
9	L-LN-CJ00041	辽宁康辉国际旅行社有限公司
10	L-ZJ-CJ00008	浙旅控股股份有限公司
11	L-BJ-WZ00011	中青旅国际旅游有限公司
12	L-SD-CJ00016	港中旅国际（山东）旅行社有限公司
13	L-HUN-CJ00008	湖南海外旅游有限公司
14	L-GD-CJ00004	广州广之旅国际旅行社股份有限公司
15	L-SD-CJ00017	山东万达国际旅行社有限公司
16	L-FJ-CJ00042	中国国旅（福建）国际旅行社有限公司
17	L-FJ-CJ00015	厦门旅游集团国际旅行社有限公司
18	L-SNX-CJ00004	陕西中国旅行社有限责任公司
19	L-FJ-CJ00011	福建康泰国际旅行社有限公司
20	L-LN-CJ00019	沈阳青年国际旅行社有限公司

2014 年度全国利税贡献二十强旅行社

位次	许可证编号	旅行社名称
1	L-SH-CJ00025	上海携程国际旅行社有限公司
2	L-BJ-CJ00071	北京众信国际旅行社股份有限公司
3	L-BJ-CJ00051	北京凯撒国际旅行社有限责任公司
4	L-GD-CJ00004	广州广之旅国际旅行社股份有限公司
5	L-BJ-CJ00043	竹园国际旅行社有限公司
6	L-CQ-CJ00001	重庆海外旅业（旅行社）集团有限公司
7	L-GD-CJ00002	广东省中国旅行社股份有限公司
8	L-HUB-CJ00019	湖北万达新航线国际旅行社有限责任公司
9	L-GD-CJ00019	广东南湖国际旅行社有限责任公司

续表

位次	许可证编号	旅行社名称
10	L-BJ-CJ00144	北京途牛国际旅行社有限公司
11	L-BJ-CJ00003	中青旅控股股份有限公司
12	L-HUN-CJ00001	湖南华天国际旅行社有限责任公司
13	L-SH-CJ00009	上海春秋国际旅行社（集团）有限公司
14	L-BJ-CJ00020	北京凤凰假期国际旅行社有限公司
15	L-FJ-CJ00020	厦门建发国际旅行社集团有限公司
16	L-FJ-CJ00002	福建省中国旅行社
17	L-SH-CJ00057	中青旅（上海）国际会议展览有限公司
18	L-SD-CJ00002	山东嘉华文化国际旅行社有限公司
19	L-ZJ-CJ00008	浙旅控股股份有限公司
20	L-BJ-CJ00001	中国国际旅行社总社有限公司

2014 年度全国旅行社集团二十强

位次	许可证编号	旅行社名称
1	L-SH-CJ00009	上海春秋国际旅行社（集团）有限公司
2	L-BJ-CJ00003	中青旅控股股份有限公司
3	L-BJ-CJ00002	中国旅行社总社有限公司
4	L-BJ-CJ00011	中国康辉旅行社集团有限责任公司
5	L-GD-CJ00002	广东省中国旅行社股份有限公司
6	L-BJ-CJ00001	中国国际旅行社总社有限公司
7	L-BJ-CJ00071	北京众信国际旅行社股份有限公司
8	L-BJ-CJ00051	北京凯撒国际旅行社有限责任公司
9	L-GD-CJ00004	广州广之旅国际旅行社股份有限公司
10	L-CQ-CJ00001	重庆海外旅业（旅行社）集团有限公司
11	L-GD-CJ00019	广东南湖国际旅行社有限责任公司
12	L-BJ-CJ00005	中信旅游集团有限公司
13	L-SH-CJ00002	上海锦江国际旅游股份有限公司
14	L-FJ10180	福建省宝中旅游集团有限公司
15	L-HUN-CJ00002	湖南省万达亲和力旅游国际旅行社有限公司
16	L-ZJ-CJ00002	浙江省中国旅行社集团有限公司
17	L-BJ-CJ00080	北京神舟国际旅行社集团有限公司
18	L-JX-CJ00007	江西光大国际旅行社有限公司
19	L-YN-CJ00020	昆明康辉旅行社有限公司
20	L-ZJ02017	浙江万达旅游集团有限公司

2014年度全国旅行社统计调查排强标准

一、百强旅行社

1. 自觉遵守国家和行业法规。经省级旅游行政管理部门审核，统计年度内未受过行政处罚、无重大安全责任事故、重大质量责任事故和重大投诉。

2. 百强旅行社排序对象为独立法人的旅行社。

3. 国内旅游组织人天、国内旅游接待人天、入境旅游外联人天、入境旅游接待人天和出境旅游组织人天五项指标中有一项进入全国前200名。

4. 在以上最多1000家旅行社中，取净资产（即所有者权益）、旅游业务营业收入（即入境、出境、国内旅游营业收入之和）、净利润（即利润总额减去所得税）、实缴税金（即营业税金及附加与所得税之和）、全部从业人员年平均人数五项指标，每项指标除以该项全国旅行社平均值得到相应系数。按五项指标相应系数之和由大到小取前100名旅行社。其中净资产、净利润小于或等于零的旅行社被排除。

5. 五项指标相应系数之和相同时，依次以旅游业务营业收入、实缴税金、净利润、净资产、人数相应系数大者为先，决定其最后排序位次。

二、入境二十强旅行社

1. 自觉遵守国家和行业法规。经省级旅游行政管理部门审核，统计年度内无重大安全责任事故、重大质量责任事故和重大投诉。

2. 入境二十强旅行社排序对象为独立法人的旅行社。

3. 入境旅游外联人天和入境旅游接待人天两项指标中有一项进入全国前 200 名。

4. 在以上最多 400 家旅行社中，取入境旅游外联人天、入境旅游接待人天、入境旅游营业收入、入境旅游营业利润、实缴税金（即营业税金及附加与所得税之和）五项指标，每项指标除以该项全国旅行社平均值得到相应系数，按五项指标相应系数之和由大到小取前 20 名旅行社。其中净资产小于或等于零的旅行社被排除。

5. 五项指标相应系数之和相同时，依次以入境旅游业务营业收入、实缴税金、入境旅游业务利润、入境旅游外联人天、入境旅游接待人天相应系数大者为先，决定其最后排序位次。

三、利税贡献二十强旅行社

1. 自觉遵守国家和行业法规。经省级旅游行政管理部门审核，统计年度内无重大安全责任事故、重大质量责任事故和重大投诉。

2. 利税贡献二十强旅行社排序对象为独立法人的旅行社。

3. 国内旅游组织人天、国内旅游接待人天、入境旅游外联人天、入境旅游接待人天和出境旅游组织人天五项指标中有一项进入全国前 200 名。

4. 在以上最多 1000 家旅行社中，按照营业税金及附加与所得税之和由大到小取前 20 名旅行社。其中净资产小于或等于零的旅行社被排除。

四、旅行社集团二十强

1. 自觉遵守国家和行业法规。经省级旅游行政管理部门审核，统计年度内未受过行政处罚、无重大安全责任事故、重大质量责任事故和重大投诉。

2. 旅行社集团二十强排序对象为合并了子公司数据的旅行社母公司。

3. 取净资产（即所有者权益）、旅游业务营业收入（即入境、出境、国内旅游营业收入之和）、净利润（即利润总额减去所得税）、实缴税金（即营业税金及附加与所得税之和）、全部从业人员年平均人数五项指标，每项指标除以该项全国旅行社平均值得到相应系数。按五项指标相应系数之和由大到小取前 10 名旅行社。其中净资产、净利润小于或等于零的旅行社被排除。

4. 五项指标相应系数之和相同时，依次以旅游业务营业收入、实缴税金、净利润、净资产、人数相应系数大者为先，决定其最后排序位次。

责任编辑：谯　洁
责任印制：冯冬青
封面设计：中文天地

图书在版编目（CIP）数据

2015中国旅行社行业发展研究报告：汉英对照 / 中华人民共和国国家旅游局编. -- 北京：中国旅游出版社，2015.12

ISBN 978-7-5032-5493-2

Ⅰ. ①2… Ⅱ. ①中… Ⅲ. ①旅行社－经济发展－研究报告－中国－2015－汉、英 Ⅳ. ①F592.6

中国版本图书馆CIP数据核字（2015）第292285号

书　　名：2015中国旅行社行业发展研究报告

作　　者：中华人民共和国国家旅游局
出版发行：中国旅游出版社
（北京建国门内大街甲9号　邮编：100005）
http://www.cttp.net.cn　E-mail:cttp@cnta.gov.cn
营销中心电话：010-85166503
经　　销：全国各地新华书店
印　　刷：北京金吉士印刷有限责任公司
版　　次：2015年12月第1版　2015年12月第1次印刷
开　　本：787毫米×1092毫米　1/16
印　　张：7.25
字　　数：60千
定　　价：58.00元
I S B N　978-7-5032-5493-2